PRAYERS FOR THE THIRD AGE

Charles Dollen

PRAYERS FOR THE THIRD AGE

A DEVOTION
FOR MATURE CATHOLICS

Rev. Charles Dollen

Our Sunday Visitor, Inc.
Huntington, Indiana 46750

International Standard Book Number:
0-87973-837-5
Library of Congress Catalog Card Number:
85-60889

Cover design by James E. McIlrath

Published, printed, and bound in the U.S.A. by
Our Sunday Visitor, Inc.
200 Noll Plaza
Huntington, Indiana 46750

837

ACKNOWLEDGMENTS

The author and publisher are grateful to the Division of Christian Education of the National Council of the Churches of Christ for the use of Scripture quotations taken from the *Revised Standard Version Bible, Catholic Edition*, © 1965 and 1966 by the Division of Christian Education of the National Council of the Churches of Christ in the U.S.A., and used by permission of the copyright owner. Among those the author and publisher are especially indebted to for material excerpted from or based on their works are: The Costello Publishing Company, Inc., for quotations taken from *Vatican II: The Conciliar and Post Conciliar Documents,* Austin Flannery, O.P., General Editor, reprinted with permission of Costello Publishing Co., Inc., © 1975 by Costello Publishing Company, Inc., and Reverend Austin Flannery, O.P., all rights reserved; Matthew Britt, *Hymns of the Breviary and Missal*, © 1922 by Burns, Oates; Bp. Charles Francis Buddy, *Thoughts of His Heart*, © 1954 by the University of San Diego Press; Abbot Columba Marmion, *Christ the Life of the Soul*, © 1924 by Sands Publishing; D.M. O'Connell, *Favorite Newman Sermons*, © 1932 by America Press; Thomas à Kempis, *The Imitation of Christ*, © 1902 by Catholic Press; St. Thomas Aquinas, *Summa Theologica*, © 1948 by Benziger; Francis Thompson's "The Hound of Heaven," in *The Book of Modern Catholic Verse*, compiled by Thomas Maynard, © 1926 by Henry Holt and Co.; and James Walsh, *Thirteenth, Greatest of Centuries*, © 1909 by Catholic Summer School Press. Other sources used in preparing this work include: *Favorite Catholic Devotions*, © 1905; *The Catholic Youth Companion*, © 1909; *The Catholic Massbook*, © 1899; and *Catholic Devotions Through the Year*, © 1901.

Dedicated to
Mary Elizabeth McKenna Portman,
a living example of
how to grow old gracefully

_____ and to _____

Michael Patrick Lyons,
her great-grandson, who has this
great legacy of love and trust

Contents

Contents

Introduction

"Grow old along with me," wrote Robert Browning. "The best is yet to be; let age approve of youth and death complete the same."

However, in our time, there is an adulation of youth that covers over the pains of growth and adolescence. Middle-aged people dress as and imitate the young with a mindless search for the mythical "fountain of youth."

This book is intended for all of us over the age of fifty who are grateful for those who patiently guided us through our young days, and happy with those who appreciate us during our middle age. Now, as we face the "third age," we hope to enjoy all that maturity can offer and we look forward with Christian joy to the promise of eternal life.

It is a mark of our maturity that we meditate on "the four last things" and prepare ourselves for the triumphant conclusion of our lives. Anything less would be the ultimate foolishness. All of our lives are a preparation for the fulfillment of our Christian hope, but in the "third age" we become more dedicated to this work.

This little manual is intended to offer help in this most important stage of our lives.

—*C.D.*

Introduction

PART 1

The Source—
Biblical Passages

The Old Testament

Psalm 23

The LORD is my shepherd, I shall not want;
　he makes me lie down in green pastures.
He leads me beside still waters;
　he restores my soul.
He leads me in paths of righteousness
　for his name's sake.
Even though I walk through the valley of the shadow
　　of death,
　I fear no evil;
for thou art with me;
　thy rod and thy staff,
　they comfort me.
Thou preparest a table before me
　in the presence of my enemies;
thou anointest my head with oil,
　my cup overflows.
Surely goodness and mercy shall follow me
　all the days of my life;
and I shall dwell in the house of the LORD
　for ever.

Wisdom 3:1-9

But the souls of the righteous are in the hand of God,
and no torment will ever touch them.
In the eyes of the foolish they seemed to have died,

and their departure was thought to be an affliction,
and their going from us to be their destruction;
but they are at peace.
For though in the sight of men they were punished,
their hope is full of immortality.
Having been disciplined a little, they will receive
    great good,
because God tested them and found them worthy of
    himself;
like gold in the furnace he tried them,
and like a sacrificial burnt offering he accepted them.
In the time of their visitation they will shine forth,
and will run like sparks through the stubble.
They will govern nations and rule over peoples,
and the Lord will reign over them for ever.
Those who trust in him will understand truth,
and the faithful will abide with him in love,
because grace and mercy are upon his elect,
and he watches over his holy ones.

Wisdom 4:7-14

But the righteous man, though he die early, will be at
    rest.
For old age is not honored for length of time,
nor measured by number of years;
but understanding is gray hair for men,
and a blameless life is ripe old age.
There was one who pleased God and was loved by
    him,

and while living among sinners he was taken up.
He was caught up lest evil change his understanding
or guile deceive his soul.
For the fascination of wickedness obscures what is
    good,
and roving desire perverts the innocent mind.
Being perfected in a short time, he fulfilled long
    years;
for his soul was pleasing to the Lord,
therefore he took him quickly from the midst of
    wickedness.

Daniel 12:1-3

"At that time shall arise Michael, the great
prince who has charge of your people. And there
shall be a time of trouble, such as never has been
since there was a nation till that time; but at that time
your people shall be delivered, every one whose name
shall be found written in the book. And many of
those who sleep in the dust of the earth shall awake,
some to everlasting life, and some to shame and
everlasting contempt. And those who are wise shall
shine like the brightness of the firmament; and those
who turn many to righteousness, like the stars for
ever and ever."

Genesis 3:14-15 (The Proto-Evangelion)

The LORD God said to the serpent,
"Because you have done this,

cursed are you above all cattle,
and above all wild animals;
upon your belly you shall go,
and dust you shall eat
all the days of your life.
I will put enmity between you and the woman,
and between your seed and her seed;
he shall bruise your head,
and you shall bruise his heel.''

Genesis 15:1-6

After these things the words of the LORD came to Abram in a vision, ''Fear not, Abram, I am your shield; your reward shall be very great.'' But Abram said, ''O Lord GOD, what wilt thou give me, for I continue childless, and the heir of my house is Eliezer of Damascus?'' And Abram said, ''Behold, thou hast given me no offspring; and a slave born in my house will be my heir.'' And behold, the word of the LORD came to him, ''This man shall not be your heir; your own son shall be your heir.'' And he brought him outside and said, ''Look toward heaven, and number the stars, if you are able to number them.'' Then he said to him, ''So shall your descendants be.'' And he believed the LORD; and he reckoned it to him as righteousness. [*Note:* Abram was later renamed Abraham by the Lord.]

Genesis 18:9-14

They said to him, "Where is Sarah your wife?" And he said, "She is in the tent." The LORD said, "I will surely return to you in the spring, and Sarah your wife shall have a son." And Sarah was listening at the tent door behind him. Now Abraham and Sarah were old, advanced in age; it had ceased to be with Sarah after the manner of women. So Sarah laughed to herself, saying, "After I have grown old, and my husband is old, shall I have pleasure?" The LORD said to Abraham, "Why did Sarah laugh, and say, 'Shall I indeed bear a child, now that I am old?' Is anything too hard for the LORD? At the appointed time I will return to you, in the spring, and Sarah shall have a son."

Genesis 21:1-4

The LORD visited Sarah as he had said, and the LORD did to Sarah as he had promised. And Sarah conceived, and bore Abraham a son in his old age at the time of which God had spoken to him. Abraham called the name of his son who was born to him, whom Sarah bore him, Isaac. And Abraham circumcised his son Isaac when he was eight days old, as God had commanded him.

Genesis 21:9-18

But Sarah saw the son of Hagar the Egyptian, whom she had borne to Abraham, playing with her son Isaac. So she said to Abraham, "Cast out this slave woman with her son; for the son of this slave woman shall not be heir with my son Isaac." And the thing was very displeasing to Abraham on account of his son. But God said to Abraham, "Be not displeased because of the lad and because of your slave woman; whatever Sarah says to you, do as she tells you, for through Isaac shall your descendants be named. And I will make a nation of the son of the slave woman also, because he is your offspring." So Abraham rose early in the morning, and took bread and a skin of water, and gave it to Hagar, putting it on her shoulder, along with the child, and sent her away. And she departed, and wandered in the wilderness of Beersheba.

When the water in the skin was gone, she cast the child under one of the bushes. Then she went, and sat down over against him a good way off, about the distance of a bowshot; for she said, "Let me not look upon the death of the child." And as she sat over against him, the child lifted up his voice and wept. And God heard the voice of the lad; and the angel of God called to Hagar from heaven, and said to her, "What troubles you, Hagar? Fear not; for God has heard the voice of the lad where he is. Arise, lift up the lad, and hold him fast with your hands; for I will make him a great nation."

Genesis 22:1-3, 6-13

After these things God tested Abraham, and said to him, "Abraham!" And he said, "Here am I." He said, "Take your son, your only son Isaac, whom you love, and go to the land of Moriah, and offer him there as a burnt offering upon one of the mountains of which I shall tell you." So Abraham rose early in the morning, saddled his ass, and took two of his young men with him, and his son Isaac; and he cut the wood for the burnt offering, and arose and went to the place of which God had told him. . . . And Abraham took the wood of the burnt offering, and laid it on Isaac his son; and he took in his hand the fire and the knife. So they went both of them together. And Isaac said to his father Abraham, "My father!" And he said, "Here am I, my son." He said, "Behold, the fire and the wood; but where is the lamb for a burnt offering?" Abraham said, "God will provide himself the lamb for a burnt offering, my son." So they went both of them together.

When they came to the place of which God had told him, Abraham built an altar there, and laid the wood in order, and bound Isaac his son, and laid him on the altar, upon the wood. Then Abraham put forth his hand, and took the knife to slay his son. But the angel of the LORD called to him from heaven, and said, "Abraham, Abraham!" And he said, "Here am I." He said, "Do not lay your hand on the lad or do anything to him; for now I know that you fear God,

seeing you have not withheld your son, your only
son, from me." And Abraham lifted up his eyes and
looked, and behold, behind him was a ram, caught in
a thicket by his horns; and Abraham went and took
the ram, and offered it up as a burnt offering instead
of his son.

Exodus 12:1-13

The LORD said to Moses and Aaron in the land of
Egypt, "This month shall be for you the beginning of
months; it shall be the first month of the year for
you. Tell all the congregation of Israel that on the
tenth day of this month they shall take every man a
lamb according to their fathers' houses, a lamb for a
household; and if the household is too small for a
lamb, then a man and his neighbor next to his house
shall take according to the number of persons;
according to what each can eat you shall make your
count for the lamb. Your lamb shall be without
blemish, a male a year old; you shall take it from the
sheep or from the goats; and you shall keep it until
the fourteenth day of this month, when the whole
assembly of the congregation of Israel shall kill their
lambs in the evening. Then they shall take some of
the blood, and put it on the two doorposts and the
lintel of the houses in which they eat them. They
shall eat the flesh that night, roasted; with
unleavened bread and bitter herbs they shall eat it.
Do not eat any of it raw or boiled with water, but

roasted, its head with its legs and its inner parts. And you shall let none of it remain until the morning, anything that remains until the morning you shall burn. In this manner you shall eat it: your loins girded, your sandals on your feet, and your staff in your hand; and you shall eat it in haste. It is the LORD's passover. For I will pass through the land of Egypt that night, and I will smite all the firstborn in the land of Egypt, both man and beast; and on all the gods of Egypt I will execute judgments: I am the LORD. The blood shall be a sign for you, upon the houses where you are; and when I see the blood, I will pass over you, and no plague shall fall upon you to destroy you, when I smite the land of Egypt."

Deuteronomy 6:1-9

"Now this is the commandment, the statutes and the ordinances which the LORD your God commanded me to teach you, that you may do them in the land to which you are going over, to possess it; that you may fear the LORD your God, you and your son and your son's son, by keeping all his statutes and his commandments, which I command you, all the days of your life; and that your days may be prolonged. Hear therefore, O Israel, and be careful to do them; that it may go well with you, and that you may multiply greatly, as the LORD, the God of your fathers, has promised you, in a land flowing with milk and honey.

"Hear, O Israel: The LORD our God is one LORD; and you shall love the LORD your God with all your heart, and with all your soul, and with all your might. And these words which I command you this day shall be upon your heart; and you shall teach them diligently to your children, and shall talk to them when you sit in your house, and when you walk by the way, and when you lie down, and when you rise. And you shall bind them as a sign upon your hand, and they shall be as frontlets between your eyes. And you shall write them on the doorposts of your house and on your gates."

Psalm 130

Out of the depths I cry to thee, O LORD!
   Lord, hear my voice!
Let thy ears be attentive
   to the voice of my supplications!
If thou, O LORD, shouldst mark iniquities,
   Lord, who could stand?
But there is forgiveness with thee,
   that thou mayest be feared.
I wait for the LORD, my soul waits,
   and in his word I hope;
my soul waits for the LORD
   more than watchmen for the morning,
   more than watchmen for the morning.
O Israel, hope in the LORD!
   For with the LORD there is steadfast love,

and with him is plenteous redemption.
And he will redeem Israel
from all his iniquities.

2 Maccabees 12:43-45

He also took up a collection, man by man, to the amount of two thousand drachmas of silver, and sent it to Jerusalem to provide for a sin offering. In doing this he acted very well and honorably, taking account of the resurrection. For if he were not expecting that those who had fallen would rise again, it would have been superfluous and foolish to pray for the dead. But if he was looking to the splendid reward that is laid up for those who fall asleep in godliness, it was a holy and pious thought. Therefore he made atonement for the dead, that they might be delivered from their sin.

Isaiah 7:10-15

Again the LORD spoke to Ahaz, "Ask a sign of the LORD your God; let it be deep as Sheol or high as heaven." But Ahaz said, "I will not ask, and I will not put the LORD to the test." And he said, "Hear then, O house of David! Is it too little for you to weary men, that you weary my God also? Therefore the Lord himself will give you a sign. Behold, a young woman shall conceive and bear a son, and shall call his name Immanuel. He shall eat curds and honey when he knows how to refuse the evil and choose the good."

Isaiah 53:1-9

Who has believed what we have heard?
   And to whom has the arm of the LORD been
     revealed?
For he grew up before him like a young plant,
   and like a root out of dry ground;
he had no form or comeliness that we should look at
   him,
   and no beauty that we should desire him.
He was despised and rejected by men;
   a man of sorrows, and acquainted with grief;
and as one from whom men hide their faces
   he was despised, and we esteemed him not.
Surely he has borne our griefs
   and carried our sorrows;
yet we esteemed him stricken,
   smitten by God, and afflicted.
But he was wounded for our transgressions,
   he was bruised for our iniquities;
upon him was the chastisement that made us whole,
   and with his stripes we are healed.
All we like sheep have gone astray;
   we have turned every one to his own way;
and the LORD has laid on him
   the iniquity of us all.
He was oppressed, and he was afflicted,
   yet he opened not his mouth;
like a lamb that is led to the slaughter,
   and like a sheep that before its shearers is dumb,

so he opened not his mouth.
By oppression and judgment he was taken away;
   and as for his generation, who considered
that he was cut off out of the land of the living,
   stricken for the transgression of my people?
And they made his grave with the wicked
   and with a rich man in his death,
although he had done no violence,
   and there was no deceit in his mouth.

Malachi 1:11

For from the rising of the sun to its setting my name is great among the nations, and in every place incense is offered to my name, and a pure offering; for my name is great among the nations, says the LORD of hosts.

Psalm 137:1-6

By the waters of Babylon, there we sat down and
   wept,
   when we remembered Zion.
On the willows there
   we hung up our lyres.
For there our captors
   required of us songs,
and our tormentors, mirth, saying,
   "Sing us one of the songs of Zion!"
How shall we sing the LORD's song
   in a foreign land?

If I forget you, O Jerusalem,
    let my right hand wither!
Let my tongue cleave to the roof of my mouth,
    if I do not remember you,
if I do not set Jerusalem
    above my highest joy!

Daniel 13:1-30, 34-64

There was a man living in Babylon whose name was Joakim. And he took a wife named Susanna, the daughter of Hilkiah, a very beautiful woman and one who feared the Lord. Her parents were righteous, and had taught their daughter according to the law of Moses. Joakim was very rich, and had a spacious garden adjoining his house; and the Jews used to come to him because he was the most honored of them all.

In that year two elders from the people were appointed as judges. Concerning them the Lord had said: "Iniquity came forth from Babylon, from elders who were judges, who were supposed to govern the people." These men were frequently at Joakim's house, and all who had suits at law came to them.

When the people departed at noon, Susanna would go into her husband's garden to walk. The two elders used to see her every day, going in and walking about, and they began to desire her. And they perverted their minds and turned away their eyes from looking to Heaven or remembering righteous judgments. Both were overwhelmed with passion for her, but they did not tell each other of their distress, for they were ashamed to disclose their lustful desire to possess her. And they watched eagerly, day after day, to see her.

They said to each other, "Let us go home, for it is mealtime." And when they went out, they parted from each other. But turning back, they met again; and when each pressed the other for the reason, they confessed their lust. And then together they arranged for a time when they could find her alone.

Once, while they were watching for an opportune day, she went in as before with only two maids, and wished to bathe in the garden, for it was very hot. And no one was there except the two elders, who had hid themselves and were watching her. she said to her maids, "Bring me oil and ointments, and shut the garden doors so that I may bathe." They did as she said, shut the garden doors, and went out by the side doors to bring what they had been commanded; and they did not see the elders, because they were hidden.

When the maids had gone out, the two elders rose and ran to her, and said: "Look, the garden doors are shut, no one sees us, and we are in love with you; so give your consent, and lie with us. If you refuse, we will testify against you that a young man was with you, and this was why you sent your maids away."

Susanna sighed deeply, and said, "I am hemmed in on every side. For if I do this thing, it is death for me; and if I do not, I shall not escape your hands. I choose not to do it and to fall into your hands, rather than to sin in the sight of the Lord."

Then Susanna cried out with a loud voice, and the two elders shouted against her. And one of them ran and opened the garden doors. When the household servants heard the shouting in the garden, they rushed in at the side door to see what had happened to her. And when the elders told their tale, the servants were greatly ashamed, for nothing like this had ever been said about Susanna.

The next day, when the people gathered at the house of her husband Joakim, the two elders came, full of their wicked plot to have Susanna put to death. They said before the people, "Send for Susanna, the daughter of Hilkiah, who is the wife of Joakim." So they sent for her. And she came, with her parents, her children, and all her kindred. . . .

Then the two elders stood up in the midst of the people, and laid their hands upon her head. And she, weeping, looked up toward heaven, for her heart trusted in the Lord. The elders said, "As we were walking in the garden alone, this woman came in with two maids, shut the garden doors, and dismissed the maids. Then a young man, who had been hidden, came to her and lay with her. We were in a corner of the garden, and when we saw this wickedness we ran to them. We saw them embracing, but we could not hold the man, for he was too strong for us, and he opened the doors and dashed out. So we seized this woman and asked her who the young man was, but she would not tell us. These things we testify."

The assembly believed them, because they were elders of the people and judges; and they condemned her to death.

Then Susanna cried out with a loud voice, and said, "O eternal God, who dost discern what is secret, who art aware of all things before they come to be, thou knowest that these men have borne false witness against me. And now I am to die! Yet I have done none of the things that they have wickedly invented against me!"

The Lord heard her cry. And as she was being led away to be put to death, God aroused the holy spirit of a young lad named Daniel; and he cried with a loud voice, "I am innocent of the blood of this woman."

All the people turned to him, and said, "What is that that you have said?" Taking his stand in the midst of them, he said, "Are you such fools, you sons of Israel? Have you condemned a daughter of Israel without examination and without learning the facts? Return to the place of judgment. For these men have borne false witness against her."

Then all the people returned in haste. And the elders said to him, "Come, sit among us and inform us, for God has given you that right." And Daniel said to them, "Separate them far from each other, and I will examine them."

When they were separated from each other, he summoned one of them and said to him, "You old relic of wicked days, your sins have now come home, which you have committed in the past, pronouncing unjust judgments, condemning the innocent and letting the guilty go free, though the Lord said, 'Do not put to death an innocent and righteous person.' Now then, if you really saw her, tell me this: Under what tree did you see them being intimate with each other?" He answered, "Under a mastic tree." And Daniel said, "Very well! You have lied against your own head, for the angel of God has received the sentence from God and will immediately cut you in two."

Then he put him aside, and commanded them to bring the other. And he said to him, "You offspring of Canaan and not of Judah, beauty has deceived you and lust has perverted your heart. This is how you both have been dealing with the daughters of Israel, and they were intimate with you through fear; but a daughter of Judah would not endure your wickedness. Now then, tell me: Under what tree did you catch them being intimate with each other?" He answered, "Under an evergreen oak." And Daniel said to him, "Very well! You also have lied against your own head, for the angel of God is waiting with his sword to saw you in two, that he may destroy you both."

Then all the assembly shouted loudly and blessed God, who saves those who hope in him. And they rose against the two elders, for out of their own mouths Daniel had convicted them of bearing false witness; and they did to them as they had wickedly planned to do to their neighbor; acting in accordance with the law of Moses, they put them to death. Thus innocent blood was saved that day.

And Hilkiah and his wife praised God for their daughter Susanna, and so did Joakim her husband and all her kindred, because nothing shameful was found in her. And from that day onward Daniel had a great reputation among the people.

Gospels

Matthew 5:1-12

Seeing the crowds, he went up on the mountain, and when he sat down his disciples came to him. And he opened his mouth and taught them, saying:

"Blessed are the poor in spirit, for theirs is the kindom of heaven.

"Blessed are those who mourn, for they shall be comforted.

"Blessed are the meek, for they shall inherit the earth.

"Blessed are those who hunger and thirst for righteousness, for they shall be satisfied.

"Blessed are the merciful, for they shall obtain mercy.

"Blessed are the pure in heart, for they shall see God.

"Blessed are the peacemakers, for they shall be called sons of God.

"Blessed are those who are persecuted for righteousness' sake, for theirs is the kingdom of heaven.

"Blessed are you when men revile you and persecute you and utter all kinds of evil against you falsely on my account. Rejoice and be glad, for your reward is great in heaven, for so men persecuted the prophets who were before you."

Matthew 11:25-30

At that time Jesus declared, "I thank thee, Father, Lord of heaven and earth, that thou hast hidden these things from the wise and understanding and revealed them to babes; yea, Father, for such was thy gracious will. All things have been delivered to me by my Father; and no one knows the Son except the Father, and no one knows the Father except the Son and any one to whom the Son chooses to reveal him. Come to me, all who labor and are heavy laden, and I will give you rest. Take my yoke upon you, and learn from me; for I am gentle and lowly in heart, and you will find rest for your souls. For my yoke is easy, and my burden is light."

Matthew 16:13-19

Now when Jesus came into the district of Caesarea Philippi, he asked his disciples, "Who do men say that the Son of man is?" And they said, "Some say John the Baptist, others say Elijah, and others Jeremiah or one of the prophets." He said to them, "But who do you say that I am?" Simon Peter replied, "You are the Christ, the Son of the living God." And Jesus answered him, "Blessed are you, Simon Bar-Jona! For flesh and blood has not revealed this to you, but my Father who is in heaven. And I tell you, you are Peter, and on this rock I will build my church, and the powers of death shall not prevail against it. I will give you the keys of the kingdom of heaven, and whatever you bind on earth shall be bound in heaven, and whatever you loose on earth shall be loosed in heaven.''

Matthew 25:31-46

[Jesus said to his disciples:] "When the Son of man comes in his glory, and all the angels with him, then he will sit on his glorious throne. Before him will be gathered all the nations, and he will separate them one from another as a shepherd separates the sheep from the goats, and he will place the sheep at his right hand, but the goats at the left. Then the King will say to those at his right hand, 'Come, O blessed of my Father, inherit the kingdom prepared for you from the foundation of the world; for I was hungry and you gave me food, I was thirsty and you gave me drink, I was a stranger and you welcomed me, I was naked and you clothed me, I was sick and you visited me, I was in prison and you came to me.' Then the righteous will answer him, 'Lord, when did we see thee hungry and feed thee, or thirsty and give thee drink? And when did we see thee a stranger and welcome thee, or naked and clothe thee? And when did we see thee sick or in prison and visit thee?' And the King will answer them, 'Truly, I say to you, as you did it to one of the least of these my brethren, you did it to me.' Then he will say to those at his left hand, 'Depart from me, you cursed, into the eternal fire prepared for the devil and his angels; for I was hungry and you gave me no food, I was thirsty and you gave me no drink, I was a stranger and you did not welcome me, naked and you did not clothe me, sick and in prison and you did not visit me.' Then they will also answer, 'Lord, when did we see thee hungry or thirsty or a stranger or naked or sick or in prison, and did not minister to thee?' Then he will answer them, 'Truly, I say to you, as you did it not to one of the least of these, you did it not to me.' And they will go away into eternal punishment, but the righteous into eternal life.''

Mark 12:28-34

And one of the scribes came up and heard them disputing with one another, and seeing that he answered them well, asked him, ''Which commandment is the first of all?'' Jesus answered, ''The first is, 'Hear, O Israel: The Lord our God, the Lord is one; and you shall love the Lord your God with all your heart, and with all your soul, and with all your mind, and with all your strength.' The second is this, 'You shall love your neighbor as yourself.' There is no other commandment greater than these.'' And the scribe said to him, ''You are right, Teacher; you have truly said that he is one, and there is no other but he; and to love him with all your heart, and with all the understanding, and with all the strength, and to love one's neighbor as oneself, is much more than all whole burnt offerings and sacrifices." And when Jesus saw that he answered wisely, he said to him, "You are not far from the kingdom of God." And after that no one dared to ask him any question.

Luke 1:26-38

In the sixth month the angel Gabriel was sent from God to a city of Galilee named Nazareth, to a virgin betrothed to a man whose name was Joseph, of the house of David; and the virgin's name was Mary. And he came to her and said, "Hail, full of grace, the Lord is with you!" But she was greatly troubled at the saying, and considered in her mind what sort of greeting this might be. And the angel said to her, "Do not be afraid, Mary, for you have found favor with God. And behold, you will conceive in your womb and bear a son, and you shall call his name Jesus.

He will be great, and will be called the Son of the
Most High;
and the Lord God will give to him the throne of
his father David,
and he will reign over the house of Jacob for
ever;
and of his kingdom there will be no end."
And Mary said to the angel, "How can this be, since I have no husband?" And the angel said to her,
"The Holy Spirit will come upon you,
and the power of the Most High will
overshadow you;

therefore the child to be born will be called holy, the Son of God.

And behold, your kinswoman Elizabeth in her age has also conceived a son; and this is the sixth month with her who was called barren. For with God nothing will be impossible." And Mary said, "Behold, I am the handmaid of the Lord; let it be to me according to your word." And the angel departed from her.

Luke 23:32-46

Two others also, who were criminals, were led away to be put to death with him. And when they came to the place which is called The Skull, there they crucified him, and the criminals, one on the right and one on the left. And Jesus said, "Father, forgive them; for they know not what they do." And they cast lots to divide his garments. And the people stood by, watching; but the rulers scoffed at him, saying, "He saved others; let him save himself, if he is the Christ of God, his Chosen One!" The soldiers also mocked him, coming up and offering him vinegar, and saying, "If you are the King of the Jews, save yourself!" There was also an inscription over him, "This is the King of the Jews."

One of the criminals who were hanged railed at him, saying, "Are you not the Christ? Save yourself and us!" But the other rebuked him, saying, "Do you not fear God, since you are under the same sentence of condemnation? And we indeed justly; for we are receiving the due reward of our deeds; but this man has done nothing wrong." And he said, "Jesus, remember me when you come in your kingly power." And he said to him, "Truly, I say to you, today you will be with me in Paradise."

It is now about the sixth hour, and there was darkness over the whole land until the ninth hour, while the sun's light failed; and the curtain of the temple was torn in two. Then Jesus, crying with a loud voice, said, "Father, into thy hands I commit my spirit!" And having said this he breathed his last.

Luke 24:1-10

But on the first day of the week, at early dawn, they went to the tomb, taking the spices which they had prepared. And they found the stone rolled away from the tomb, but when they went in they did not find the body. While they were preplexed about this, behold, two men stood by them in dazzling apparel; and as they were frightened and bowed their faces to the ground, the men said to them, "Why do you seek the living among the dead? He is not here, but has risen. Remember how he told you, while he was still in Galilee, that the Son of man must be delivered into the hands of sinful men, and be crucified, and on the third day rise." And they remembered his words, and returning from the tomb they told all this to the eleven and to all the rest. Now it was Mary

Magdalene and Joanna and Mary the mother of
James and the other women with them who told this
to the apostles.

John 1:1-18

In the beginning was the Word, and the Word
was with God, and the Word was God. He was in the
beginning with God; all things were made through
him, and without him was not anything made that
was made. In him was life, and the life was the light
of men. The light shines in the darkness, and the
darkness has not overcome it.

There was a man sent from God, whose name
was John. He came for testimony, to bear witness to
the light, that all might believe through him. He was
not the light, but came to bear witness to the light.

The true light that enlightens every man was
coming into the world. He was in the world, and the
world was made through him, yet the world knew
him not. He came to his own home, and his own
people received him not. But to all who received him,
who believed in his name, he gave power to become
children of God; who were born, not of blood nor of
the will of the flesh nor of the will of man, but of
God.

And the Word became flesh and dwelt among
us, full of grace and truth; we have beheld his glory,
glory as of the only Son from the Father. (John bore
witness to him, and cried, "This was he of whom I

said, 'He who comes after me ranks before me, for he was before me.' ") And from his fulness have we all received, grace upon grace. For the law was given through Moses; grace and truth came through Jesus Christ. No one has ever seen God; the only Son, who is in the bosom of the Father, he has made him known.

John 6:35, 37-40

Jesus said to them, "I am the bread of life; he who comes to me shall not hunger, and he who believes in me shall never thirst. . . . All that the Father gives me will come to me; and him who comes to me I will not cast out. For I have come down from heaven, not to do my own will, but the will of him who sent me; and this is the will of him who sent me, that I should lose nothing of all that he has given me, but raise it up at the last day. For this is the will of my Father, that every one who sees the Son and believes in him should have eternal life; and I will raise him up at the last day."

John 6:51-58

I am the living bread which came down from heaven; if any one eats of this bread, he will live for ever; and the bread which I shall give for the life of the world is my flesh."

The Jews then disputed among themselves, saying, "How can this man give us his flesh to eat?"

So Jesus said to them, "Truly, truly, I say to you, unless you eat the flesh of the Son of man and drink his blood, you have no life in you; he who eats my flesh and drinks my blood has eternal life, and I will raise him up at the last day. For my flesh is food indeed, and my blood is drink indeed. He who eats my flesh and drinks my blood abides in me, and I in him. As the living Father sent me, and I live because of the Father, so he who eats me will live because of me. This is the bread which came down from heaven, not such as the fathers ate and died; he who eats this bread will live for ever."

John 11:17-27

Now when Jesus came, he found that Lazarus had already been in the tomb four days. Bethany was near Jerusalem, about two miles off, and many of the Jews had come to Martha and Mary to console them concerning their brother. When Martha heard that Jesus was coming, she went and met him, while Mary sat in the house. Martha said to Jesus, "Lord, if you had been here, my brother would not have died. And even now I know that whatever you ask from God, God will give you." Jesus said to her, "Your brother will rise again." Martha said to him, "I know that he will rise again in the resurrection at the last day." Jesus said to her, "I am the resurrection and the life; he who believes in me, though he die, yet shall he live, and whoever lives and believes in me shall never die. Do you believe this?'' She said to him, ''Yes, Lord; I believe that you are the Christ, the Son of God, who is coming into the world.''

John 12:23-28

And Jesus answered them, ''The hour has come for the Son of man to be glorified. Truly, truly, I say to you, unless a grain of wheat falls into the earth and dies, it remains alone; but if it dies, it bears much fruit. He who loves his life loses it, and he who hates his life in this world will keep it for eternal life. If any one serves me, he must follow me; and where I am, there shall my servant be also: if any one serves me, the Father will honor him.

''Now is my soul troubled. And what shall I say? 'Father, save me from this hour'? No, for this purpose I have come to this hour. Father, glorify thy name.'' Then a voice came from heaven, ''I have glorified it, and I will glorify it again.''

John 13:31-35

When he had gone out, Jesus said. ''Now is the Son of man glorified, and in him God is glorified; if God is glorified in him, God will also glorify him in himself, and glorify him at once. Little children, yet a little while I am with you. You will seek me; and as I said to the Jews so now I say to you; 'Where I am going you cannot come.' A new commandment I give to you, that you love one another; even as I have loved you, that you also love one another. By this all men will know that you are my disciples, if you have love for one another."

John 20:11-18

But Mary stood weeping outside the tomb, and as she wept she stooped to look into the tomb; and she saw two angels in white, sitting where the body of Jesus had lain, one at the head and one at the feet. They said to her, "Woman, why are you weeping?" She said to them, "Because they have taken away my Lord, and I do not know where they have laid him." Saying this, she turned round and saw Jesus standing, but she did not know that it was Jesus. Jesus said to her, "Woman, why are you weeping? Whom do you seek?" Supposing him to be the gardener, she said to him, "Sir, if you have carried him away, tell me where you have laid him, and I will take him away." Jesus said to her, "Mary." She turned and said to him in Hebrew, "Rabboni!" (which means Teacher). Jesus said to her, "Do not hold me, for I have not yet ascended to the Father; but go to my brethren and say to them, I am ascending to my Father and your Father, to my God and your God." Mary Magdalene went and said to the disciples, "I have seen the Lord"; and she told them that he had said these things to her.

John 20:24-29

Now Thomas, one of the twelve, called the Twin, was not with them when Jesus came. So the other disciples told him, "We have seen the Lord." But he said to them, "Unless I see in the hands the print of the nails, and place my finger in the mark of the nails, and place my hand in his side, I will not believe."

Eight days later, his disciples were again in the house, and Thomas was with them. The doors were shut, but Jesus came and stood among them, and said, "Peace be with you." Then he said to Thomas, "Put your finger here, and see my hands; and put out your hand, and place it in my side; do not be faithless, but believing." Thomas answered him, "My Lord and my God!" Jesus said to him, "Have you believed because you have seen me? Blessed are those who have not seen and yet believe."

John 21:24-25

This is the disciple who is bearing witness to these things, and who has written these things; and we know that his testimony is true.

But there are also many other things which Jesus did; were every one of them to be written, I suppose that the world itself could not contain the books that would be written.

Acts of the Apostles

Acts 3:1-8

Now Peter and John were going up to the temple at the hour of prayer, the ninth hour. And a man lame from birth was being carried, whom they laid daily at the gate of the temple which is called Beautiful to ask alms of those who entered the temple. Seeing Peter and John about to go into the temple, he asked for alms. And Peter directed his gaze at him, with John, and said, "Look at us." And he fixed his attention upon them, expecting to receive something from them. But Peter said, "I have no silver and gold, but I give you what I have; in the name of Jesus Christ of Nazareth, walk." And he took him by the right hand and raised him up; and immediately his feet and ankles were made strong. And leaping up he stood and walked and entered the temple with them, walking and leaping and praising God.

Acts 9:1-19

But Saul, still breathing threats and murder against the disciples of the Lord, went to the high priest and asked him for letters to the synagogues at Damascus, so that if he found any belonging to the Way, men or women, he might bring them bound to Jerusalem. Now as he journeyed he approached

Damascus, and suddenly a light from heaven flashed about him. And he fell to the ground and heard a voice saying to him, "Saul, Saul, why do you persecute me?" And he said, "Who are you, Lord?" And he said, "I am Jesus, whom you are persecuting; but rise and enter the city, and you will be told what you are to do." The men who were traveling with him stood speechless, hearing the voice but seeing no one. Saul arose from the ground; and when his eyes were opened, he could see nothing; so they led him by the hand and brought him into Damascus. And for three days he was without sight, and neither ate nor drank.

Now there was a disciple at Damascus named Ananias. The Lord said to him in a vision, "Ananias." And he said, "Here I am, Lord." And the Lord said to him, "Rise and go to the street called Straight, and inquire in the house of Judas for a man of Tarsus named Saul; for behold, he is praying, and he has seen a man named Ananias come in and lay his hands on him so that he might regain his sight." But Ananias answered, "Lord, I have heard from many about this man, how much evil he has done to thy saints at Jerusalem; and here he has authority from the chief priests to bind all who call upon thy name." But the Lord said to him, "Go, for he is a chosen instrument of mine to carry my name before the Gentiles and kings and the sons of Israel; for I will show him how much he must suffer for the sake of my name." So Ananias departed and entered the house. And laying his hands on him he said, "Brother Saul, the Lord Jesus who appeared to you on the road by which you came, has sent me that you may regain your sight and be filled with the Holy Spirit." And immediately something like scales fell from his eyes and he regained his sight. Then he rose and was baptized, and took food and was strengthened.

Epistles and Revelation

Romans 5:5-11

Hope does not disappoint us, because God's love has been poured into our hearts through the Holy Spirit who has been given to us.

While we were yet helpless, at the right time Christ died for the ungodly. Why, one will hardly die for a righteous man — though perhaps for a good man one will dare even to die. But God shows his love for us in that while we were yet sinners Christ died for us. Since, therefore, we are now justified by his blood, much more shall we be saved by him from the wrath of God. For if while we were enemies we were reconciled to God by the death of his Son, much more, now that we are reconciled, shall we be saved by his life. Not only so, but we also rejoice in God through our Lord Jesus Christ, through whom we have now received our reconciliation.

Romans 5:17-21

If, because of one man's trespass, death reigned through that one man, much more will those who receive the abundance of grace and the free gift of righteousness reign in life through the one man Jesus Christ.

Then as one man's trespass led to condemnation for all men, so one man's act of righteousness leads to acquittal and life for all men. For as by one man's disobedience many were made sinners, so by one man's obedience many will be made righteous. Law came in, to increase the trespass; but where sin increased, grace abounded all the more, so that, as sin reigned in death, grace also might reign through righteousness to eternal life through Jesus Christ our Lord.

Romans 6:3-11

Do you not know that all of us who have been baptized into Christ Jesus were baptized into his death? We were buried therefore with him by baptism into death, so that as Christ was raised from the dead by the glory of the Father, we too might walk in newness of life.

For if we have been united with him in a death like this, we shall certainly be united with him in a resurrection like his. We know that our old self was crucified with him so that the sinful body might be destroyed, and we might no longer be enslaved to sin. For he who has died is freed from sin. But if we have died with Christ, we believe that we shall also live with him. For we know that Christ being raised from the dead will never die again; death no longer has dominion over him. The death he died he died to sin, once for all, but the life he lives he lives to God. So you also must consider yourselves dead to sin and alive to God in Christ Jesus.

Romans 8:14-17

For all who are led by the Spirit of God are sons of God. For you did not receive the spirit of slavery to fall back into fear, but you have received the spirit of sonship. When we cry, "Abba! Father!" it is the Spirit himself bearing witness with our spirit that we are children of God, and if children, then heirs, heirs of God and fellow heirs with Christ, provided we suffer with him in order that we may also be glorified with him.

Romans 14:7-12

None of us lives to himself, and none of us dies to himself. If we live, we live to the Lord, and if we die, we die to the Lord; so then, whether we live or whether we die, we are the Lord's. For to this end Christ died and lived again, that he might be Lord both of the dead and of the living.

Why do you pass judgment on your brother? Or you, why do you despise your brother? For we shall all stand before the judgment seat of God; for it is written,

"As I live, says the Lord, every knee shall bow to
   me,
and every tongue shall give praise to God."

So each of us shall give account of himself to God.

1 Corinthians 11:23-29

For I received from the Lord what I also delivered to you, that the Lord Jesus on the night when he was betrayed took bread, and when he had given thanks, he broke it, and said, "This is my body which is for you. Do this in remembrance of me." In the same way also the cup, after supper, saying, "This cup is the new covenant in my blood. Do this, as often as you drink it, in remembrance of me." For as often as you eat this bread and drink the cup, you proclaim the Lord's death until he comes.

Whoever, therefore, eats the bread or drinks the cup of the Lord in an unworthy manner will be guilty of profaning the body and blood of the Lord. Let a man examine himself, and so eat of the bread and drink of the cup. For any one who eats and drinks without discerning the body eats and drinks judgment upon himself.

1 Corinthians 13

If I speak in the tongues of men and of angels, but have not love, I am a noisy gong or a clanging cymbal. And if I have prophetic powers, and understand all mysteries and all knowledge, and if I have all faith, so as to remove mountains, but have not love, I am nothing. If I give away all I have, and if I deliver my body to be burned, but have not love, I gain nothing.

Love is patient and kind; love is not jealous or

boastful; it is not arrogant or rude. Love does not insist on its own way; it is not irritable or resentful; it does not rejoice at wrong, but rejoices in the right. Love bears all things, believes all things, hopes all things, endures all things.

Love never ends; as for prophecies, they will pass away; as for tongues, they will cease; as for knowledge, it will pass away. For our knowledge is imperfect and our prophecy is imperfect; but when the perfect comes, the imperfect will pass away. When I was a child, I spoke like a child, I thought like a child, I reasoned like a child; when I became a man, I gave up childish ways. For now we see in a mirror dimly, but then face to face. Now I know in part; then I shall understand fully, even as I have been fully understood. So faith, hope, love abide, these three; but the greatest of these is love.

1 Corinthians 15:20-28

But in fact Christ has been raised from the dead, the first fruits of those who have fallen asleep. For as by a man came death, by a man has come also the resurrection of the dead. For as in Adam all die, so also in Christ shall all be made alive. But each in his own order: Christ the first fruits, then at his coming those who belong to Christ. Then comes the end, when he delivers the kingdom to God the Father after destroying every rule and every authority and power. For he must reign until he has put all his enemies under his feet. The last enemy to be destroyed is death. "For God has put all things in subjection under his feet." But when it says, "All things are put in subjection under him," it is plain that he is excepted who put all things under him. When all things are subjected to him, then the Son himself will also be subjected to him who put all things under him, that God may be everything to every one.

2 Corinthians 5:1, 6-10

For we know that if the earthly tent we live in is destroyed, we have a building from God, a house not made with hands, eternal in the heavens. . . . So we are always of good courage; we know that while we are at home in the body we are away from the Lord, for we walk by faith, not by sight. We are of good courage, and we would rather be away from the body and at home with the Lord. So whether we are at home or away, we make it our aim to please him. For we must all appear before the judgment seat of Christ, so that each one may receive good or evil, according to what he has done in the body.

Galatians 6:14-18

But far be it from me to glory except in the cross of our Lord Jesus Christ, by which the world has been crucified to me, and I to the world. For neither circumcision counts for anything, nor uncircumcision, but a new creation. Peace and mercy be upon all who walk by this rule, upon the Israel of God.

Henceforth let no man trouble me; for I bear on my body the marks of Jesus.

The grace of our Lord Jesus Christ be with your spirit, brethren. Amen.

Ephesians 1:3-10, 22

Blessed be the God and Father of our Lord Jesus Christ, who has blessed us in Christ with every spiritual blessing in the heavenly places, even as he chose us in him before the foundation of the world, that we should be holy and blameless before him. He destined us in love to be his sons through Jesus Christ, according to the purpose of his will, to the praise of his glorious grace which he freely bestowed on us in the Beloved. In him we have redemption through his blood, the forgiveness of our trespasses, according to the riches of his grace which he lavished upon us. For he has made known to us in all wisdom and insight the mystery of his will, according to his purpose which he set forth in Christ as a plan for the fulness of time, to unite all things in him, things in heaven and things on earth. . . . He has put all things under his feet and has made him the head over all things for the church.

Ephesians 3:14-21

For this reason I bow my knees before the
Father, from whom every family in heaven and on
earth is named, that according to the riches of his
glory he may grant you to be strengthened with
might through his Spirit in the inner man, and that
Christ may dwell in your hearts through faith: that
you, being rooted and grounded in love, may have
power to comprehend with all the saints what is the
breadth and length and height and depth, and to
know the love of Christ which surpasses knowledge,
that you may be filled with all the fulness of God.

Now to him who by the power at work within
us is able to do far more abundantly than all that we
ask or think, to him be glory in the church and in
Christ Jesus to all generations, for ever and ever.
Amen.

Philippians 2:5-11

Have this mind among yourselves, which was in
Christ Jesus, who, though he was in the form of God,
did not count equality with God a thing to be
grasped, but emptied himself, taking the form of a
servant, being born in the likeness of men. And being
found in human form he humbled himself and
became obedient unto death, even death on a cross.
Therefore God has highly exalted him and bestowed
on him the name which is above every name, that at
the name of Jesus every knee should bow, in heaven

and on earth and under the earth, and every tongue confess that Jesus Christ is Lord, to the glory of God the Father.

Colossians 1:15-20

He is the image of the invisible God, the first-born of all creation; for in him all things were created, in heaven and on earth, visible and invisible, whether thrones or dominions or principalities or authorities — all things were created through him and for him. He is before all things, and in him all things hold together. He is the head of the body, the church; he is the beginning, the first-born from the dead, that in everything he might be pre-eminent. For in him all the fulness of God was pleased to dwell, and through him to reconcile to himself all things, whether on earth or in heaven, making peace by the blood of his cross.

Colossians 3:1-4

If then you have been raised with Christ, seek the things that are above, where Christ is, seated at the right hand of God. Set your minds on things that are above, not on things that are on earth. For you have died, and your life is hid with Christ in God. When Christ who is our life appears, then you also will appear with him in glory.

Hebrews 1:1-4

In many and various ways God spoke of old to our fathers by the prophets; but in these last days he has spoken to us by a Son, whom he appointed the heir of all things, through whom also he created the world. He reflects the glory of God and bears the very stamp of his nature, upholding the universe by his word of power. When he had made purification for sins, he sat down at the right hand of the Majesty on high, having become as much superior to angels as the name he has obtained is more excellent than theirs.

James 2:14-26

What does it profit, my brethren, if a man says he has faith but has not works? Can his faith save him? If a brother or sister is ill-clad and in lack of daily food, and one of you says to them, "Go in peace, be warmed and filled," without giving them the things needed for the body, what does it profit? So faith by itself, if it has no works, is dead.

But some one will say, "You have faith and I have works." Show me your faith apart from your works, and I by my works will show you my faith. You believe that God is one; you do well. Even the demons believe — and shudder. Do you want to be shown, you foolish fellow, that faith apart from works is barren? Was not Abraham our father justified by works, when he offered his son Isaac upon the altar? You see that faith was active along with his works, and faith was completed by works, and the scripture was fulfilled which says, "Abraham believed God, and it was reckoned to him as righteousness"; and he was called the friend of God. You see that a man is justified by works and not by faith alone. And in the same way was not also Rahab the harlot justified by works when she received the messengers and sent them out another way? For as the body apart from the spirit is dead, so faith apart from works is dead.

1 Peter 2:19-25

For one is approved if, mindful of God, he endures pain while suffering unjustly. For what credit is it, if when you do wrong and are beaten for it you take it patiently? But if when you do right and suffer for it you take it patiently, you have God's approval. For to this you have been called, because Christ also suffered for you, leaving you an example, that you should follow in his steps. He committed no sin; no guile was found on his lips. When he was reviled, he did not revile in return; when he suffered, he did not threaten; but he trusted to him who judges justly. He himself bore our sins in his body on the tree, that we might die to sin and live to righteousness. By his wounds you have been healed. For you were straying like sheep, but have now returned to the Shepherd and Guardian of your souls.

1 John 3:1-2

See what love the Father has given us, that we should be called children of God; and so we are. The reason why the world does not know us is that it did not know him. Beloved, we are God's children now; it does not yet appear what we shall be, but we know that when he appears we shall be like him, for we shall see him as he is.

1 John 4:7-12

Beloved, let us love one another; for love is of God, and he who loves is born of God and knows God. He who does not love does not know God; for God is love. In this the love of God was made manifest among us, that God sent his only Son into the world, so that we might live through him. In this is love, not that we loved God but that he loved us and sent his Son to be the expiation of our sins. Beloved, if God so loved us, we also ought to love one another. No man has ever seen God; if we love one another, God abides in us and his love is perfected in us.

Revelation 14:13

And I heard a voice from heaven saying, "Write this: Blessed are the dead who die in the Lord henceforth." "Blessed indeed," says the Spirit, "that they may rest from their labors, for their deeds follow them!"

Revelation 21:1-7

Then I saw a new heaven and a new earth; for the first heaven and the first earth had passed away, and the sea was no more. And I saw the holy city, new Jerusalem, coming down out of heaven from God, prepared as a bride adorned for her husband; and I heard a great voice from the throne saying, "Behold, the dwelling of God is with men. He will dwell with them, and they shall be his people, and God himself will be with them; he will wipe away every tear from their eyes, and death shall be no more, neither shall there be mourning nor crying nor pain any more, for the former things have passed away."

And he who sat upon the throne said, "Behold, I make all things new." Also he said, "Write this, for these words are trustworthy and true." And he said to me, "It is done! I am the Alpha and the Omega, the beginning and the end. To the thirsty I will give water without price from the fountain of the water of life. He who conquers shall have this heritage, and I will be his God and he shall be my son."

PART 2

Lift Up Your Hearts—
Favorite and Familiar Prayers

The Holy Trinity

A Prayer of Cardinal Francis Spellman

Most Holy Trinity, be forever blessed by our prayers and praise, for the greater glory of your name and the salvation of souls.

O God the Father, giver of life, grant to praying souls the grace of life to do your will.

O God the Son, giver of light, grant to praying minds the grace of light to know your truth.

O God the Holy Spirit, giver of love, grant to praying hearts the grace of love to live in your love. Amen.

A Prayer of St. Gregory Nazianzen

Lord Jesus, you want us to become a living force for all mankind — lights shining in the world. You want us to become radiant lights as we stand beside you, the great light, bathed in your glory, O Light of Heaven.

Let us enjoy, more and more, the pure and dazzling light of the Holy Trinity, as now we have received, though not in its fullness, a ray of its splendor, proceeding from the one true God, in Christ Jesus, our Lord, to whom be power and glory for ever and ever. Amen.

A Prayer of St. Catherine of Siena

Eternal God, eternal Trinity, you have made the Blood of Christ so precious through his sharing in your divine nature. You are a mystery as deep as the sea; the more I search, the more I find, and the more I find, the more I search for you.

I can never be satisfied; what I receive will ever leave me desiring more. When you fill my soul I have an even greater hunger and I grow more famished for your light. I desire above all else to see you, the true light, as you really are.

You are my creator, eternal Trinity, and I am your creature. You have made me a new creation in the Blood of your Son, and I know that you are moved with love at the beauty of your creation.

I know that you are beauty and wisdom itself. The food of angels, you gave yourself to us in the fire of your love, O Triune God! Amen.

Prayers of Faith, Hope, and Love

• O my God, I believe that you are one God in three divine persons, the Father, the Son, and the Holy Spirit. I believe that your divine Son became man and died for our salvation, and that he will come again to judge the living and the dead. I believe these and all the truths taught by the Catholic Church because you have revealed them. Amen.

• O my God, relying on your infinite goodness and compassion, I hope to obtain pardon for my sins, the help of your grace, and life everlasting, through the merits of our Lord and Savior, Jesus Christ. Amen.

• O my God, I love you above all things, with my whole heart and soul, because you are infinite goodness and worthy of all love. I love my neighbor as myself for love of you. I forgive all who have injured me and ask pardon of all whom I may have offended. Amen.

Prayers to the Holy Trinity

• Most Holy Trinity, Godhead indivisible of the Father, the Son, and the Holy Spirit, our first beginning and our last end! Since you have made us in your own image and likeness, grant that all the thoughts of our minds, all the words of our tongues, all the affection of our hearts, and all our actions may be always conformed to your most holy will, so that, after having witnessed you through your works here on earth, and seen you in a dark manner by means of faith, we may come at last to contemplate you face to face in perfect possession of you forever in paradise. Amen.

• Almighty and everlasting God, you have granted to us, your servants, in the profession of the true faith, to acknowledge the glory of the eternal Trinity, and, in the power of your majesty, to adore the Unity; grant, we ask you, that by steadfastness in the same faith, we may always be defended from all adversity. Through Christ, our Lord. Amen.

A Morning Prayer

O God, I offer you this day
   All that I'll think or do or say,
Uniting it with what was done
   On earth by Jesus Christ, your Son.

A Prayer of T.B. DeView

Lord, may your will be done,
   whether I sit or stand or go.
Lord, may your will be done,
   though it bring me gain or woe.
Lord, may your will be done,
   though the reason for it I may not know.

Acts of Contrition

   • O my God, I am heartily sorry for having offended you, and I detest all my sins because of your just punishments, but especially because they offend you, my God, who are so good and so deserving of all love. I firmly resolve, with the help of your grace, to sin no more and to avoid the near occasions of sin. Amen.

   • O my God, I am sorry for having offended you because you are so good and so deserving of love. I love you above all things. Grant me the courage and wisdom to avoid sin. Amen.

The 'Gloria'

Glory to God in the highest,
    and peace to his people on earth.
Lord God, heavenly King,
almighty God and Father,
    we worship you, we give you thanks,
    we praise you for your glory.
Lord Jesus Christ, only Son of the Father,
Lord God, Lamb of God,
you take away the sin of the world:
    have mercy on us;
you are seated at the right hand of the Father:
    receive our prayer.
For you alone are the Holy One,
you alone are the Lord,
you alone are the Most High,
    Jesus Christ,
    with the Holy Spirit,
    in the glory of God the Father. Amen.

A Prayer for Prosperity

O God, my creator, you have given me talents to
be put to use. Help me use them to support those
whom I love and to reach my own goals. Grant me
industry and wisdom, patience and prudence,
generosity and fairness. Let me serve you by serving
others and to build up a treasure in heaven. Amen.

The 'Te Deum'

You are God, we praise you;
You are the Lord: we acclaim you;
You are the eternal Father:
All creation worships you.

To you all angels, all the powers of heaven,
Cherubim and Seraphim sing in endless praise:
  Holy, holy, holy Lord, God of power and might,
  Heaven and earth are full of your glory.

The glorious company of apostles praise you.
The noble fellowship of prophets praise you.
The white-robed army of martyrs praise you.

Throughout the world Holy Church acclaims you:
  Father of majesty unbounded,
  Your true and only Son, worthy of all worship,
  And the Holy Spirit, advocate and guide.
You, Christ, are the king of glory,
The eternal Son of the Father.
When you became man to set us free
You did not spurn the virgin's womb.
You overcame the sting of death
And opened the kingdom of heaven to all believers.
You are seated at God's right hand in glory.
We believe that you will come and be our judge.

Come then, Lord, and help your people,
Bought with the price of your own blood,
And bring us with your saints to glory everlasting.
  Amen.

The 'Benedictus'

Blessed be the Lord, the God of Israel;
He has come to his people and set them free.
He has raised up for us a mighty savior,
Born of the house of his servant David.
Through his prophets he promised of old
That he would save us from our enemies,
From the hands of all who hate us.
He promised to show mercy to our fathers
And to remember his holy covenant.
This was the oath he swore to our father Abraham:
To set us free from the hands of our enemies,
Free to worship him without fear,
Holy and righteous in his sight
All the days of our lives.
You, my child, shall be called the prophet of the Most
    High;
For you will go before the Lord to prepare his way.
To give his people knowledge of salvation
By the forgiveness of sins.
In the tender compassion of our God
The dawn from on high shall break upon us,
To shine on those who dwell in darkness and the
    shadow of death,
And to guide our feet into the way of peace. Amen.

A Prayer Attributed to St. Patrick

Christ be with me, Christ before me,
Christ be after me, Christ within me,

Christ beneath me, Christ above me,
Christ at my right hand, Christ at my left,
Christ in the fort, Christ in the chariot,
Christ in the ship,
Christ in the heart of every man who thinks of me,
Christ in the mouth of every man who speaks of me,
Christ in every ear that hears me.
May the strength of God pilot us.
May the power of God preserve us.
May the wisdom of God instruct us.
May the hand of God protect us.
May the way of God direct us.
May the shield of God defend us.
May the host of God guard us against the snares of
the Evil One and the temptations of the world.
Amen.

A Morning Offering

O Jesus, through the Immaculate Heart of
Mary, I offer you my prayers, works, joys, and
sufferings of this day, for all the intentions of your
Sacred Heart, in union with the holy sacrifice of the
Mass throughout the world, in reparation for my
sins, in reparation for all sins, for the intentions of all
of our associates, and in particular for_____
_____. Amen.

Prayer Before a Crucifix

Look down upon me, good and gentle Jesus, while before your face I humbly kneel, while with burning affection I pray and beg you to fix deep in my heart a lively sentiment of faith, hope, and charity, true contrition for my sins, and a firm purpose of amendment. I contemplate with great love and pity your five most precious wounds, pondering over them within me, while I call to mind the words which David the prophet said of you, my Jesus: They have pierced my hands and my feet; they have numbered all my bones.

Anima Christi*

Soul of Christ, sanctify me.
Body of Christ, save me.
Blood of Christ, inebriate me.
Water from the side of Christ, wash me.
Passion of Christ, strengthen me.
Good Jesus, hear me.
Within your wounds, hide me.
Suffer me not to be separated from you.
From the malicious enemy defend me.
In the hour of my death call me,
And bid me come to you, that with your saints I may
        praise you for ever and ever. Amen.

---

*Said to be the favorite prayer of St. Ignatius Loyola.

Prayers to the Most Blessed Sacrament

• May the Heart of Jesus in the Most Blessed Sacrament be praised, adored, and loved in all the tabernacles of the world, with grateful affection, even to the end of time. Amen.

• O my Lord and my God, you are infinitely good. Give to me all those graces of which I stand in need. O most loving Jesus, strengthen and bless me by the power of the Most Blessed Sacrament, now and at the hour of my death. Amen.

The Divine Praises

Blessed be God.
Blessed be his holy name.
Blessed be Jesus Christ, true God and true man.
Blessed be the name of Jesus.
Blessed be his most sacred heart.
Blessed be his most precious blood.
Blessed be Jesus in the most holy sacrament of the
    altar.
Blessed be the Holy Spirit, the Paraclete.
Blessed be the great mother of God, Mary most holy.
Blessed be her holy and immaculate conception.
Blessed be her glorious assumption.
Blessed be the name of Mary, virgin and mother.
Blessed be St. Joseph, her most chaste spouse.
Blessed be God in his angels and in his saints.

Litany of the Sacred Heart of Jesus

Lord, have mercy on us.

Christ, have mercy on us.

Lord, have mercy on us.

Christ, hear us.

Christ, graciously hear us.

God the Father of heaven, *[after each invocation, the response is:] have mercy on us.*

God the Son, Redeemer of the world,

God the Holy Spirit,

Holy Trinity, one God,

Heart of Jesus, Son of the eternal Father,

Heart of Jesus, formed by the Holy Spirit in the womb of the Virgin Mother,

Heart of Jesus, substantially united to the Word of God,

Heart of Jesus, of infinite majesty,

Heart of Jesus, sacred temple of God,

Heart of Jesus, tabernacle of the Most High,

Heart of Jesus, house of God and gate of heaven,

Heart of Jesus, burning furnace of charity,

Heart of Jesus, abode of justice and love,

Heart of Jesus, full of goodness and love,

Heart of Jesus, abyss of all virtues,

Heart of Jesus, most worthy of all praise,

Heart of Jesus, king and center of all hearts,

Heart of Jesus, in whom are all the treasures of wisdom and knowledge,

Heart of Jesus, in whom dwells the fullness of
divinity,
Heart of Jesus, in whom the Father was well pleased,
Heart of Jesus, of whose fullness we have all
received,
Heart of Jesus, desire of the everlasting hills,
Heart of Jesus, patient and most merciful,
Heart of Jesus, enriching all who invoke you,
Heart of Jesus, fountain of life and holiness,
Heart of Jesus, propitiation for our sins,
Heart of Jesus, loaded down with opprobrium,
Heart of Jesus, bruised for our offenses,
Heart of Jesus, obedient unto death,
Heart of Jesus, pierced with a lance,
Heart of Jesus, source of all consolation,
Heart of Jesus, our life and resurrection,
Heart of Jesus, our peace and reconciliation,
Heart of Jesus, victim for our sins,
Heart of Jesus, salvation of those who trust in you,
Heart of Jesus, hope of those who die in you,
Heart of Jesus, delight of all the saints,

Lamb of God, who take away the sins of the world,
spare us, O Lord.
Lamb of God, who take away the sins of the world,
graciously hear us, O Lord.
Lamb of God, who take away the sins of the world,
have mercy on us.

V. Jesus, meek and humble of heart,
R. *Make our hearts like your very own.*

Let us pray: O almighty and eternal God, look upon the heart of your dearly beloved Son, and upon the praise and satisfaction he offers you in behalf of sinners, and being appeased, grant pardon to those who seek your mercy, in the name of the same Jesus Christ, your Son, who lives and reigns with you, in the unity of the Holy Spirit, world without end. Amen.

The Great Promises of the Sacred Heart
(As revealed to
St. Margaret Mary Alacoque)

[The Sacred Heart of Jesus favored St. Margaret Mary Alacoque with many apparitions. He encouraged devotion to his Sacred Heart and included these twelve promises for those who would undertake this devotion.]

1. I will give them all the graces necessary for their state in life.

2. I will grant peace to their families.

3. I will console them in all their troubles.

4. I will be their sure refuge during life and particularly at the hour of their death.

5. I will abundantly bless all their undertakings.

6. Sinners will find in my Heart an infinite ocean of mercy.

7. Tepid souls shall become fervent.

8. Fervent souls shall rise rapidly to great perfection.

9. I will bless the houses where an image of my Sacred Heart is exposed and honored.

10. I will give to priests the gift of touching the most hardened of hearts.

11. Those who propagate this devotion shall have their names written in my Heart, never to be effaced.

12. To those who receive Holy Communion on the first Friday for nine consecutive months, I promise the grace of final perseverance; they shall not die in my disfavor nor without receiving the sacraments, and my Heart shall be their refuge at the last hour.

"Behold this Heart, which has loved mankind so much!"

The Way of the Cross
*(Composed and edited
by Sebastian W. Pfeiffer)*

• **Introduction**
Lord Jesus, help us accompany you in your journey up to Calvary. As you, the innocent one,

take up this heavy burden of the cross, help us poor sinners as we try to carry our daily crosses.

We remember your promise to make the yoke sweet and the burden light. Help us imitate you, whose example was one who was meek and humble of heart. Through your sufferings, death, and resurrection, help us have the courage and the wisdom to face life each day.

- **First Station: Jesus is condemned to death**

V. We adore you, O Christ, and we praise you.

R. Because by your holy cross you have redeemed the world.

Meditation: Condemned and spurned by the elders of your own people, you are hastened before Pontius Pilate for the death sentence. Even this bored and jaded pagan can find no guilt in you, but he hands you over to the Roman soldiers for crucifixion.

Prayer: How often we may have deserved the death sentence for our sins. You, Lord Jesus, have taken the cruel burden of our sins on yourself — the innocent for the sinner, the just for the unjust. Jesus, meek and humble of heart, make our hearts like unto your own. Amen.

(A verse of the "Stabat Mater" may be prayed or sung after each Station.)

Jesus, Lord, condemned, defiled,
May we, too, be meek and mild
As we tread your holy way.

- **Second Station: Jesus takes up his cross**

V. We adore you, O Christ, and we praise you.

R. Because by your holy cross you have redeemed the world.

Meditation: The Roman form of execution was not a pretty or merciful thing at all. Crucifixion was designated for slaves to deter rebellion, and it was prolonged as much as possible. Christ, weakened by the scourging and the crowning with thorns, is brought exhausted to carry his own cross up the long hill.

Prayer: Lord Jesus, you still carry your cross in your persecuted brothers and sisters around the world. Help us reach out to all who suffer the loss of their human rights or their human dignity. Help us to carry our own crosses each day in union with you. Amen.

> May we feel no bitter hatred,
> When we, too, are persecuted,
> Left alone to walk with you.

- **Third Station: Jesus falls the first time**

V. We adore you, O Christ, and we praise you.

R. Because by your holy cross you have redeemed the world.

Meditation: After the Last Supper, Christ went to the Garden of Gethsemane to pray. He knew the agony ahead of him. After the arrest and trial, he was

tortured and then started on the journey to Golgotha.
In his exhaustion he fell under the wood of the cross.

Prayer: Lord Jesus, to save us from sin and
eternal despair, you embraced this cross and
embarked on this fearsome journey. Help us embrace
the baptismal graces you have given us and go
forward in your strength on the journey of life.
Amen.

> Weakened, prodded, cursed, and fallen,
> His whole body bruised and swollen,
> Jesus tripped and lay in pain.

• **Fourth Station: Jesus meets his afflicted Mother**

V. We adore you, O Christ, and we praise you.

R. Because by your holy cross you have
redeemed the world.

Meditation: The prophet Simeon had warned
the Blessed Mother that a sword of sorrow would
pierce her soul. How that prophecy was fulfilled on
Christ's passage to Calvary! Who could describe or
fully understand the emotions that passed between
Mother and Son in this hour?

Prayer: Christ, you are the Man of Sorrows
described by the prophets of the Old Testament. You
have chosen to share your saving work with all of us,
but in first place is your Mother, the Woman of
Sorrows. Mary, sorrowful Mother, intercede for us
with your divine Son. Amen.

Jesus met his grieving Mother,
She who made the Lord our brother;
Now the sword her heart has pierced.

- **Fifth Station: Simon of Cyrene helps Jesus carry his cross**

V. We adore you, O Christ, and we praise you.

R. Because by your holy cross you have redeemed the world.

Meditation: Afraid that Jesus would die before he reached Calvary's heights, the Roman [soldiers] forced a certain Simon of Cyrene to help Jesus carry the cross. Did Simon ever come to realize the privilege that was his?. . .

Prayer: Lord Jesus, your grace helps us to carry our crosses during our life here on earth. Help us to see and respond to those around us who carry heavy burdens. Amen.

Simon stopped in hesitation,
Not foreseeing his proud station,
Called to bear the cross of Christ.

- **Sixth Station: Veronica wipes the face of Jesus**

V. We adore you, O Christ, and we praise you.

R. Because by your holy cross you have redeemed the world.

Meditation: Veronica was noble because of her courage, her sympathy, and her daring. What love it took to face the jeering crowds to perform this service for Christ.

Prayer: Lord Jesus, you told us that when we serve the poor and the weak, the least of the brethren, we are serving you. Do not let us grow weary in performing the spiritual and corporal works of mercy. Make our faith come alive through the works of charity. Amen.

> Brave but trembling came the woman,
> None but she would flaunt the Roman,
> Moved by love beyond her fear.

• Seventh Station: Jesus falls the second time

V. We adore you, O Christ, and we praise you.

R. Because by your holy cross you have redeemed the world.

Meditation: Though he was true God, he was also truly a man, and in his human nature he suffered bitterly. As the crowd roared, and with soldiers swearing, his exhausted body falls again to the ground. They did not recognize him who is "God from God, Light from Light, true God from true God." Would we have recognized him — do we recognize him today?

Prayer: Lord Jesus, help me recognize you in all who turn to me in need. Let me support you in them with my words and deeds. In turn, strengthen me in the vocation you have given me, that I may return to you as a good and faithful steward. Amen.

Prostrate on the ground he crumbled,
Flogged in body he resembled
All our brethren poor and scorned.

- **Eighth Station: Jesus meets the women of Jerusalem**

V. We adore you, O Christ, and we praise you.

R. Because by your holy cross you have redeemed the world.

Meditation: These holy women of Jerusalem were a credit to our race. Where were the men who had listened to him and witnessed his miracles? These womanly tears were a priceless testimony to their love.

Prayer: Lord Jesus, have pity on our brothers and sisters who are sick and poor, broken down by indifference and the greed of others, or beaten down by injustice. Give us the grace to stand up for them whenever the opportunity offers itself. Amen.

May our sympathy for Jesus
Turn to those who here now need us,
May we see Christ bruised in them.

- **Ninth Station: Jesus falls the third time**

V. We adore you, O Christ, and we praise you.

R. Because by your holy cross you have redeemed the world.

Meditation: Our Holy Redeemer, agonized and bruised, falls yet again. It appeared that the end had approached; but, no, he struggles to his feet again to continue the final few steps to Golgotha.

Prayer: Lord Jesus, we have fallen into sin again and again, yet your mercy endures forever. You call sinners to conversion and when they lift themselves from sin, you invite them into the warmth of your own Sacred Heart. Forgive us, Lord; strengthen us for the glory of your name. Amen.

> Jesus fell again in weakness,
> Stumbling as we do, to lead us
> Through our sorrow and our pain.

• Tenth Station: Jesus is stripped of his garments

V. We adore you, O Christ, and we praise you.

R. Because by your holy cross you have redeemed the world.

Meditation: The vile executioners stripped Jesus of his clothes. The pain of this ordeal, which took large portions of flesh that had adhered to his blood-soaked garments, was offered in expiation for our many sins. Christ suffered this indignity to cover the coldness and nakedness of our hearts.

Prayer: Lord Jesus, you were naked before your enemies, powerless in the hands of sinners. Clothe us with a genuine love of all and do not let our hearts ever be filled with hatred or bitterness. Amen.

> Stripped and jeered by his own nation,
> Jesus stood in desolation,
> Giving all he had to give.

• Eleventh Station: Jesus is nailed to the cross

V. We adore you, O Christ, and we praise you.

R. Because by your holy cross you have redeemed the world.

Meditation: When they came to Golgotha, the Place of the Skull, they crucified Jesus between two thieves, one to his right and the other to his left. He endured the excruciating torture of having his hands and feet brutally nailed to the wood of the cross.

Prayer: Lord Jesus, you reminded us that we must take up our crosses daily to follow you. Let us grow in faith, hope, and love so that we may embrace the crosses and burdens in our daily lives. The royal road of the cross leads certainly to the risen life. Amen.

> Pierced the hands that blessed and cured us,
> Pierced the feet that walked to free us,
> Walked the hill of Calvary.

• Twelfth Station: Jesus dies on the cross

V. We adore you, O Christ, and we praise you.

R. Because by your holy cross you have redeemed the world.

Meditation: The ignominy, the folly of the cross! In this supreme sacrifice of love our Lord offered himself for the salvation of the world. He is the Lamb of God who takes away the sins of the world. Through his death we have all been justified.

God the Father accepts this total act of love for the redemption of our whole human race.

Prayer: Lord Jesus, help us to understand more fully this total and supreme act of love. Through your obedience to your Father's will you have given us the example to follow. Make this sacrifice fruitful in our lives. Amen.

> Life eternal, death defiant,
> Bowed his head — the world was silent,
> Through his death came life anew.

• **Thirteenth Station: Jesus is taken down from the cross**

V. We adore you, O Christ, and we praise you.

R. Because by your holy cross you have redeemed the world.

Meditation: Mary his Mother stood at the foot of the cross, a witness to the crucifixion. How tenderly she must have received that broken body into her arms. How the memories of Bethlehem, Nazareth, and Cana must have washed through her mind. Joseph of Arimathea arranged for a hasty burial.

Prayer: Lord Jesus, when all seems to fail, when we are deserted by our friends, help us remember that the darkness on Calvary led surely and swiftly to the glory of the resurrection. Be our safe refuge throughout our lives. Amen.

Stunned and stricken, Mary, Mother,
In your arms was placed our brother,
"Full of grace" now filled with grief.

- **Fourteenth Station: Jesus is laid in the tomb**

V. We adore you, O Christ, and we praise you.

R. Because by your holy cross you have
redeemed the world.

Meditation: A small band of close disciples
gathered around as Jesus was sealed into the
borrowed tomb. How complete and thorough their
desolation must have been. All their hopes, all their
goals, all their dreams, were washed against the huge
stone rolled over the entrance. And then the soldiers
came to guard the tomb.

Prayer: Lord Jesus, let us keep vigil before this
tomb, remembering that the trials and tribulations of
this life are as nothing compared to the life that
awaits us in heaven. The price of our redemption was
not the blood of goats or heifers, but the precious
blood of the God-Man. Amen.

Jesus, Lord, your gift accepted,
In three days you resurrected,
You did first what we shall do.

- **Fifteenth Station: The resurrection**

V. We adore you, O Christ, and we praise you.

R. Because by your holy cross you have
redeemed the world.

Meditation: What an incredible day that first

Easter Sunday was! Viewed from the part of the apostles it was staggering and then triumphant. Once again, it was the love and faith of the woman on that early Sunday morn that brings joy to our hearts. And, it is piously believed that the Blessed Virgin Mary rejoiced in his presence for the entire final forty days of Christ's life on earth.

Prayer: Lord Jesus, help us glory in the name "Christian," for we have been called to be, and we are, children of God. Help us live lives worthy of so high a calling. Amen.

> Jesus risen, be our lover
> In your Food and in our brother.
> Lead us home to heaven with you.

Novena to the Sacred Heart

O Most holy Heart of Jesus, fountain of every blessing, I adore you, I love you, and with a lively sorrow for my sins, I offer you this poor heart of mine.

Make me humble and patient, and wholly obedient to your will. Grant, good Jesus, that I may live in you and for you.

Protect me in the midst of dangers; comfort me in my afflictions; give me health of body and mind, assistance in my temporal needs; grant your blessing on all that I do, and the grace of a holy death. Amen.

Eucharistic Salutation

O sacrament most holy,
O sacrament divine,
All praise and all thanksgiving
Be every moment thine.

A Prayer of St. Francis of Assisi

I believe that you are present in the Blessed
Sacrament, O Jesus. I love you and desire you. Come
into my heart.

I embrace you; O never leave me. I beg you, O
Lord Jesus, that the burning and most sweet power of
your love absorb my mind, that I may die through
love of your love, since you graciously died for love
of my love.

The 'Pange Lingua'
(St. Thomas Aquinas)

Sing, my tongue, the Savior's glory,
    Of his flesh the mystery sing:
Of the blood, all price exceeding,
    Shed by our immortal king.
Destined for the world's redemption,
    From a noble womb to spring.

Of a pure and spotless virgin,
    Born for us on earth below,
He, as man, with man conversing,
    Stayed the seeds of truth to sow;

Then he closed in solemn order
  Wondrously his life of woe.

On the night of that last supper,
  Seated with his chosen band,
He, the paschal victim eating,
  First fulfills the law's command:
Then as food to all his brethren
  Gives himself with his own hand.

Word made flesh, the bread of nature
  By his word to flesh he turns;
Wine into his blood he changes:
  What though sense no change discerns?
Only be the heart in earnest,
  Faith her lesson quickly learns.

A Prayer of St. Ambrose

Come, Holy Spirit, who ever one
Are with the Father and the Son;
It is the hour, our soul possess
With your full flood of holiness.

Let flesh and heart and lips and mind
Sound forth our witness to mankind;
And love light up our mortal frame,
Till others catch the living flame.

Grant this, O Father, ever one,
With Christ, your sole-begotten Son,
And Holy Spirit, whom all adore,
Reigning and blest forevermore.

A Prayer to the Holy Spirit

Give me grace, O Holy Spirit, Spirit of the Father and the Son, to say to you always and everywhere, "Speak, Lord, for your servant is listening."

Spirit of wisdom, preside over all my thoughts, words, and actions, from this hour until the moment of my death.

Spirit of understanding, enlighten and teach me.

Spirit of counsel, direct my inexperience.

Spirit of fortitude, strengthen my weakness.

Spirit of knowledge, instruct my ignorance.

Spirit of piety, make me fervent in all good works.

Spirit of fear of the Lord, restrain me from all evil.

The 'Veni, Creator'

Come, Holy Spirit, creator blest,
    And in our hearts take up your rest.
Come with your grace and heavenly aid
    To fill the hearts which you have made.

O Great Paraclete, to you we cry;
    O highest gift of God most high!
O fount of life, O fire of love,
    And sweet anointing from above!

You in your sevenfold gifts are known.
    You, the finger of God's right hand we own.

You are the promise of the Father
    Who endow the tongue with speech.

Kindle our senses from above,
    And make our hearts overflow with love;
With patience firm and virtue high,
    The weakness of our flesh supply.

Far from us drive the foe we dread,
    And grant us your true peace instead;
So shall we not, with you as guide,
    Turn from the path of life aside.

O may your grace on us bestow,
    The Father and the Son to know.
And you, through endless time confessed,
    Of both the eternal Spirit blest.

The 'Veni, Sancte Spiritus'

Come, Holy Spirit, come,
    From your bright and glorious throne
        Rays of healing light impart.

Come, O Father of the poor,
    Source of gifts that will endure,
        Light of every human heart.

You of all consolers best,
    Of the soul most kindly guest,
        Life-giving courage to bestow.

In hard labor you are rest,
   In the heat you refresh the best,
      And solace give us in our woe.

O most blessed light divine,
   Let your radiance in us shine,
      And our inmost being fill.

Nothing good by man is thought,
   Nothing right by him is wrought,
      When he spurns your gracious will.

Cleanse our souls from sinful stain,
   Wash our dryness with your rain,
      Heal our wounds and mend our ways.

Bend the stubborn heart and will,
   Melt the frozen, warm the chill,
      Guide the steps that go astray.

On the faithful who in you
   Trust with child-like piety,
      Deign your sevenfold gift to send.

Give them virtue's rich increase,
   Saving grace to die in peace,
      Give them joys that never end. Amen.

A Prayer of Jacques Bénigne Bossuet

Almighty God, eternal God, blessed God, I rejoice in your almighty power, your eternity, and your blessedness. When shall I behold you, O

Principle without principle! When shall I behold your Son, equal to yourself, coming forth from your bosom! When shall I behold your Holy Spirit proceeding from this union, being the term of your fruitfulness and consummating your eternal action!

An Act of Consecration
(Abbot Columba Marmion, O.S.B.)

O eternal Father, prostrate in humble adoration at your feet, we consecrate our whole being to the glory of your Son, Jesus, the Word Incarnate. You have established him as king of our souls; submit to him our souls, our hearts, our bodies; let nothing in us move except by his orders, except by his inspiration.

United with him, may we be born into your bosom and consummated in the unity of your love. O Jesus, unite us to yourself in your life of perfect sanctity, wholly consecrated to your Father and to souls. Be our wisdom, our justice, our sanctification, our redemption, our all. Sanctify us in truth.

O Holy Spirit, love of the Father and the Son, establish yourself as a furnace of love in the center of our hearts and bear constantly upwards, like eager flames, our thoughts, our affections, and our actions even to the bosom of the Father. May our entire life be a *Gloria Patri et Filio et Spiritui Sancto*.

O Mary, Mother of Christ, Mother of fair love, form us according to the heart of your Son.

Prayer to the Spirit of Truth

O Holy Spirit of God, take me as your disciple.
   Guide me,
   Illuminate me,
   Sanctify me.

Bind my hands that they may do no evil;
Cover my eyes that they may see it no more;
Sanctify my heart that evil may not dwell within me.

Be my God; be my guide.
Wherever you lead me, I shall go,
Whatever you forbid me, I will renounce;
Whatever you command me, in your strength, I will
   do.

Lead me, then, into the fullness of your truth. Amen.

The Blessed Virgin Mary

A Prayer of St. Venantius Fortunatus

The God whom earth and sea and sky
Adore and laud and magnify,
Whose might they own, whose praise they tell,
In Mary's body deigned to dwell.

O Mother blest! the chosen shrine
Wherein the architect divine,
Whose hand contains the earth and sky,
Vouchsafed in hidden guise to lie.

Blest in the message Gabriel brought,
Blest in the work the Spirit wrought,
Most blest to bring to human birth,
The long-desired of all the earth.
O Lord, the virgin born, to you
Eternal praise and glory be.
Whom with the Father we adore
And Holy Spirit for ever more. Amen.

The 'Alma Redemptoris Mater'

O Loving Mother of the Redeemer,
Gate of Heaven and Star of the Sea,
Assist your people who have fallen, yet strive to rise
    again.
To the wonderment of nature, you bore your
    Creator,

Yet remained a virgin, after as before.
You who received Gabriel's joyful greeting,
Have pity on us poor sinners.

The 'Memorare'

Remember, O most gracious Virgin Mary, that never was it known, that anyone who fled to your protection, sought your help and begged your intercession, was left unaided.

Inspired by this confidence, we fly unto you, O Virgin of virgins, our mother. To you do we come, before you we kneel, sinful and sorrowful.

O Mother of the Word Incarnate, despise not our petitions, but in your clemency, hear and answer us. Amen.

The 'Magnificat' (Luke 1:46-55)

My soul magnifies the Lord,
and my spirit rejoices in God my Savior,
For he has regarded the low estate of his handmaiden.
For behold, henceforth all generations will call me
    blessed;
for he who is mighty has done great things for me,
and holy is his name.
And his mercy is on those who fear him
from generation to generation.
He has shown strength with his arm,
he has scattered the proud in the imagination of their
    hearts,

he has put down the mighty from their thrones,
and exalted those of low degree;
he has filled the hungry with good things,
and the rich he has sent empty away.
He has helped his servant Israel,
in remembrance of his mercy,
as he spoke to our fathers,
to Abraham and to his posterity for ever.

The 'Angelus'

The angel of the Lord declared unto Mary:
And she conceived of the Holy Spirit.
    Hail Mary. . .

Behold the handmaid of the Lord:
Be it done unto me according to your word.
    Hail Mary. . .

And the Word was made flesh:
And dwelt among us.
    Hail Mary. . .

Pray for us, O holy Mother of God,
That we may be made worthy of the promises of
    Christ.

    Let us pray: Pour forth, we ask you, O Lord,
your grace into our hearts, that we, to whom the
incarnation of Christ, your Son, was made known by
the message of an angel, may by his passion and
cross, be brought to the glory of his resurrection.
Through the same Christ, our Lord. Amen.

Litany of Loreto*

Lord, have mercy on us.

Christ, have mercy on us.

Lord, have mercy on us.

Christ, hear us.

Christ, graciously hear us.

God the Father of heaven, *have mercy on us.*

God the Son, Redeemer of the world, *have mercy on us.*

God the Holy Spirit, *have mercy on us.*

Holy Trinity, one God, *have mercy on us.*

Holy Mary, *[after each invocation, the response is:] pray for us.*

Holy Mother of God,

Holy Virgin of virgins,

Mother of Christ,

Mother of divine grace,

Mother most pure,

Mother most chaste,

Mother inviolate,

Mother undefiled,

Mother most amiable,

Mother most admirable,

Mother of good counsel,

Mother of our Creator,

---

*St. Peter Canisius popularized this ancient devotion to the Blessed Virgin Mary throughout Europe.

Mother of our Savior,
Virgin most prudent,
Virgin most venerable,
Virgin most renowned,
Virgin most powerful,
Virgin most merciful,
Virgin most faithful,
Mirror of justice,
Seat of wisdom,
Cause of our joy,
Spiritual vessel,
Vessel of honor,
Singular vessel of devotion,
Mystical rose,
Tower of David,
Tower of ivory,
House of gold,
Ark of the covenant,
Gate of heaven,
Morning star,
Health of the sick,
Refuge of sinners,
Comforter of the afflicted,
Help of Christians,
Queen of angels,
Queen of patriarchs,
Queen of prophets,
Queen of apostles,
Queen of martyrs,

Queen of confessors,
Queen of virgins,
Queen of all saints,
Queen conceived without original sin,
Queen assumed into heaven,
Queen of the most holy Rosary,
Queen of peace,

Lamb of God, who take away the sins of the world,
     spare us, O Lord.
Lamb of God, who take away the sins of the world,
     graciously hear us, O Lord.
Lamb of God, who take away the sins of the world,
     have mercy on us.
     V. Pray for us, O Holy Mother of God,
     R. *That we may be made worthy of the promises*
of Christ.

     Let us pray: Grant us your servants, we beg you,
O Lord God, to enjoy perpetual health of mind and
body, that through the glorious intercession of
blessed Mary, ever virgin, we may be delivered from
present sorrow, and enjoy everlasting happiness.
Through the same Christ, our Lord. Amen.

Rosary Meditations
(Joseph Benedict)

THE JOYFUL MYSTERIES

• The First Joyful Mystery: The Annunciation

The Archangel Gabriel appeared to Mary and greeted her joyfully, "Hail, full of grace, the Lord is with you." He told her of God's plan for her to become the Mother of God. He also told her that her Son was to be named "Jesus." Then all heaven and earth waited for her humble *fiat* — "Be it done unto me according to your word."

"In God's will is our peace" (Dante).

• The Second Joyful Mystery: The Visitation

Gabriel told Mary that her kinswoman Elizabeth was to have a child in her old age. Mary hastened into the hill country to share with her relatives the marvelous fulfillment of all the Old Testament promises. St. Elizabeth proclaimed, "Blessed are you among women!" Mary responded with the *Magnificat*, a song of praise to God who is faithful in all his deeds.

"Your faith is proclaimed in all the world" (Romans 1:8).

• The Third Joyful Mystery: The Nativity

"There was a census throughout the whole world," and Joseph and his wife went to Bethlehem of Judea to be counted. There, in a manger, Jesus was born of the Virgin. The heavens exploded in angelic song and the shepherds hastened to adore, followed by the Magi, the Wise Men.

"O come, let us adore him: Christ, the Lord."

• The Fourth Joyful Mystery: The Presentation

According to the Law of Moses, the Child had to be presented in the Temple. With what heart-filled joy Mary and Joseph must have entered the Temple that day. The Temple's Lord was making his first appearance there, "his Father's house." Simeon makes his prophecy over the Child and over the Mother:

"You shall call his name Jesus, for he will save his people from their sins" (Matthew 1:21).

• The Fifth Joyful Mystery: Finding Jesus in the Temple

Obeying the Law of Moses faithfully, Joseph and Mary took Jesus to the Temple when he was approaching adolescence. He was inadvertently left behind, and the pair returned in haste to look for him. Joseph and Mary found him in the Temple, talking with the teachers. How anxious Jesus was to begin work on "his Father's business."

"Make love your aim. . ." (1 Corinthians 14:1).

- **The First Sorrowful Mystery: The Agony in the Garden**

    After giving his Church the gift of the Eucharist, Christ knew that his passion and death were at hand. He went to the Garden of Gethsemane to pray for the courage to do his Father's will. The apostles slept through much of this, even the beloved Peter, James, and John. Judas and the powers of evil were to have their short triumph.

    "Not what I will, but what thou wilt" (Mark 14:36).

- **The Second Sorrowful Mystery: The Scourging at the Pillar**

    The drama of the passion continued after the arrest of Jesus. He was hauled before Pontius Pilate and Herod and back to Pilate. He had come to bear witness to the truth, but they could not stand it. Pilate ordered the brutal Roman punishment of the scourging. The bloodbath continued.

    "Blood of Christ, inebriate me!" (*Anima Christi*).

- **The Third Sorrowful Mystery: The Crowning With Thorns**

    While his enemies spent a busy night plotting his death, Christ was being tormented by the cruel Roman guards. He had said he was a king, so they made him a crown of thorns and pressed the terrible spikes into his head. He took upon himself the price of our sins.

"A man of sorrows . . . from whom men hide their faces. . ." (Isaiah 53:3).

• The Fourth Sorrowful Mystery: The Carrying of the Cross

Condemned to death, Jesus made the journey along the Via Dolorosa. Every step was painful. He stumbled and fell, and he accepted the help of Simon the Cyrenian. He saw his Mother and the women of Jerusalem. Then he was at Golgotha, the Place of the Skull, and his body was thrown on the wood of the cross and nailed there.

"At the cross, her station keeping,
Stood the mournful mother, weeping. . ."
(Stabat Mater).

• The Fifth Sorrowful Mystery: The Crucifixion

This most cruel death was the price Christ paid for our salvation. It was a supreme act of obedience to his Father's will; it was the one complete and total sacrifice of love. Through the sacrifice of the Mass it is made present in our lives over and over again, until the Lord returns to judge the living and the dead.

"Christ also died for sins once for all. . ." (1 Peter 3:18).

THE GLORIOUS MYSTERIES

- **The First Glorious Mystery: The Resurrection**

    Early on that first Easter Sunday, Jesus rose, glorious and immortal. Once again, the angels announced his triumph. Mary Magdalene is caught up in this mystery, and then the apostles, and the disciples on their way to Emmaus. For forty days he stayed with them, teaching them the things of the kingdom. (Many spiritual writers think that Mary enjoyed his presence throughout the forty days.)

    Alleluia, Alleluia, he is risen as he said!

- **The Second Glorious Mystery: The Ascension**

    At the end of his earthly life, Jesus ascended into heaven. Before he left his followers he commissioned them to go out into the whole world and make disciples of all peoples. They were to baptize in the name of the Holy Trinity: in the name of the Father, the Son, and the Holy Spirit.

    Jesus will return in splendor (see Acts 1:11).

- **The Third Glorious Mystery: The Descent of the Holy Spirit**

    Christ promised that he would not leave his disciples as orphans, but little did they suspect the greatness of the gift he would send them. On Pentecost, ten days after his Ascension, he sent the Holy Spirit upon them, the fire of love and the Advocate, or Paraclete. In this spirit they set out to evangelize the whole world. It's a work in which we share, until the end of time.

"Regeneration and renewal in the Holy Spirit" (Titus 3:5).

• The Fourth Glorious Mystery: The Assumption of Mary

At the end of her earthly sojourn, Mary was taken body and soul into heaven. Because of her Immaculate Conception, she was free from sin and the wages of original sin, the pain of death and bodily corruption. No city so sacred nor any shrine, however venerable, has ever claimed to have the body of the Blessed Mother.

"Whether we live or whether we die, we are the Lord's" (Romans 14:8).

• The Fifth Glorious Mystery: The Coronation of Mary as Queen of Heaven

Christ welcomed Mary into heaven where she reigns forever with him. She is the daughter of God the Father, Mother of the Son of God, and spouse of the Holy Spirit. Saints, poets, artists, and theologians have vied with each other in trying to describe the glory of this event. It can only be understood as a mystery of love.

"Hail, full of grace, the Lord is with you!"

Concluding prayers for the Rosary:

Hail, holy Queen, Mother of mercy: hail, our life, our sweetness, and our hope. To you do we cry, poor banished children of Eve. To you do we send up our sighs, mourning and weeping in this vale of tears. Turn, then, most gracious advocate, your eyes of mercy toward us. And after this, our exile, show unto us the blessed fruit of your womb, Jesus. O clement, O loving, O sweet Virgin Mary.

Pray for us, O Queen of the Most Holy Rosary,
That we may be made worthy of the promises of Christ.

Let us pray: O God whose only-begotten Son, by his life, death, and resurrection, has purchased for us the joys of eternal life, grant, we beg you, that meditating on these mysteries of the most holy Rosary of the Blessed Virgin Mary, we may imitate what they contain and obtain what they promise, through the same Christ, our Lord. Amen.

The 'Dignare Me, Laudare Te'

Vouchsafe that I may praise you, O holy Virgin;
Give me strength against your enemies.

The 'Sub Tuum Praesidium'

We fly to your patronage, O holy Mother of God; despise not our petitions in our necessities, but deliver us always from all dangers, O glorious and blessed Virgin. Amen.

The 'Regina Caeli'

O Queen of heaven, rejoice, alleluia,
For he whom you merited to bear, alleluia,
Has risen as he said, alleluia.

V. Rejoice and be glad, O Virgin Mary, alleluia,
R. *Because the Lord is truly risen, alleluia.*

Let us pray: O God, who by the resurrection of your Son, our Lord Jesus Christ, has brought joy to the whole world, grant that through the intercession of the Virgin Mary, his Mother, we may lay hold of the joys of eternal life. Through the same Christ, our Lord. Amen.

The 'Tota Pulchra Es'

You are all fair, O Mary.
The original stain is not in you.
You are the glory of Jerusalem,
The joy of Israel,
The great honor of our race,
The advocate of sinners.
O Mary, O Mary,
Virgin most prudent,
Mother most merciful,
Pray for us,
Intercede for us with our Lord Jesus Christ. Amen.

A Prayer to Our Lady of Guadalupe

Our Lady of Guadalupe, mystical rose, intercede for Holy Church, protect the Holy Father, help all who turn to you in their needs, and, since you are the ever Virgin Mary and Mother of the true God, obtain for us from your most holy Son, the grace of keeping our faith, sweet hope in the midst of the trials of life, burning charity, and the precious gift of final perseverance. Amen.

A Prayer to Our Mother of Good Counsel

O most gracious Virgin Mary, Mother of Good Counsel, chosen by the eternal Counsel to be the Mother of the eternal Word made flesh, to you who are the treasurer of divine graces and the advocate of sinners, I who am your most unworthy servant have recourse: be my guide and counselor in this vale of tears, obtain for me through the most precious blood of your divine Son, the forgiveness of my sins, the salvation of my soul, and the means necessary to obtain it. In like manner, obtain for Holy Church victory over her enemies and the spread of the kingdom of Jesus Christ throughout the whole earth. Amen.

A Prayer to Our Lady of Refuge

Almighty and merciful God, who in blessed Mary ever Virgin has set up a refuge and a help for sinners, grant that we, under her protection and through her intercession, may be absolved from all our sins and may obtain the blessed effect of your great mercy. Through Christ our Lord. Amen.

The Angels and Saints

A Prayer to All the Angels

All you holy angels and archangels, thrones and dominations, principalities and powers, the virtues of the heavens, cherubim and seraphim, praise the Lord for ever. Amen.

A Prayer to One's Guardian Angel

O angel of God, my guardian dear,
To whom his love commits me here,
Ever this day be at my side,
To watch and guard, to rule and guide. Amen.

A Prayer to St. Michael the Archangel

St. Michael the Archangel, defend us in battle, be our protection against the wiles and snares of the devil; may God rebuke him, we humbly pray; and do you, O prince of the heavenly hosts, by the power of God, thrust into hell Satan and all other evil spirits who wander through the world seeking the ruin of souls. Amen.

A Prayer in Honor of the Archangel Gabriel

O God, who from among all your angels chose the Archangel Gabriel to announce the mystery of the Incarnation, mercifully grant that we who solemnly remember him on earth may feel the benefit

of his patronage in heaven, who lives and reigns for
ever and ever. Amen.

A Prayer for the Archangel Raphael's Help

O God, send the Archangel Raphael to our
assistance. May he who stands for ever praising you
at your throne present our humble petitions to be
blessed by you. Through Christ our Lord. Amen.

A Prayer for St. Joseph's Intercession and Protection

O God, in your eternal providence you chose St.
Joseph to be the spouse of your most holy Mother;
grant that we may deserve to have him as our
intercessor in heaven even as we venerate him as our
protector on earth, who lives and reigns, world
without end. Amen.

A Prayer to St. Joseph as Patron and Defender

O glorious St. Joseph, chosen by God to be the
foster-father of Jesus, the chaste spouse of Mary ever
Virgin, and head of the Holy Family, be the heavenly
patron and defender of the Church founded by Jesus.

With confidence we beg your powerful aid for
the Church on earth. Shield it with paternal love,
especially the Supreme Pontiff together with all the
bishops and priests who are in union with the Holy

See of Peter. Be the defender of all who labor for souls.

Protect the working men and women and their families. Intercede for young people who are searching for their place in life. Be the sure refuge for all of us at the hour of our death and guide us safely into heaven. In Jesus' name we pray. Amen.

Litany of St. Joseph
Lord, have mercy on us.
Christ, have mercy on us.
Lord, have mercy on us.
Christ, hear us.
Christ, graciously hear us.
God the Father of heaven, *have mercy on us.*
God the Son, Redeemer of the world, *have mercy on us.*
God the Holy Spirit, *have mercy on us.*
Holy Trinity, one God, *have mercy on us.*
Holy Mary, *[after each invocation, the response is:] pray for us.*
St. Joseph,
Renowned offspring of David,
Light of patriarchs,
Spouse of the Mother of God,
Chaste guardian of the Virgin,
Foster-father of the Son of God,
Diligent protector of Christ,
Head of the Holy Family,

Joseph most just,
Joseph most chaste,
Joseph most prudent,
Joseph most strong,
Joseph most obedient,
Joseph most faithful,
Mirror of patience,
Lover of poverty,
Model of artisans,
Glory of home life,
Guardian of virgins,
Solace of the wretched,
Hope of the sick,
Patron of the dying,
Terror of demons,
Protector of Holy Church,

Lamb of God, who take away the sins of the world,
    spare us, O Lord.
Lamb of God, who take away the sins of the world,
    graciously hear us, O Lord.
Lamb of God, who take away the sins of the world,
    have mercy on us.
    V. He made him Lord over his house:
    R. *And ruler of all his substance.*

Let us pray: O God, in your divine wisdom and
providence, you chose St. Joseph to be the spouse of
the Blessed Mother and the earthly protector of your
Son, Jesus Christ. Grant that we may deserve to have

him as our intercessor in heaven, since we venerate him on earth as our protector too. In Jesus' name we pray. Amen.

A Prayer to St. Peter

You are the shepherd of the sheep, the prince of the apostles; you were given the keys of the kingdom of heaven.

V. You are Peter,

R. *And upon this Rock I will build my Church.*

Let us pray: Raise us up, we ask you, O Lord, by the apostolic assistance of blessed Peter, your apostle, so that the weaker we are, the more mightily we may be helped by the power of his intercession, and that being perpetually defended by the name of the holy apostle, we may neither yield to any evil nor be overcome by any adversity. Through Christ our Lord. Amen.

A Prayer to St. Paul the Apostle

You are the vessel of election, St. Paul the Apostle, the preacher of the truth in the whole world.

V. Pray for us, St. Paul the Apostle,

R. *That we may be made worthy of the promises of Christ.*

Let us pray: Almighty and everlasting God, in your divine mercy you instructed your blessed Apostle Paul what he should do that he might be filled with the Holy Spirit; with his admonitions directing and by his merits interceding for us, grant that we may serve you in holy fear and trembling and so be filled with the comfort of your heavenly gifts, through Christ our Lord. Amen.

A Prayer of St. Francis

Make me, O Lord, an instrument of your peace.
Where there is hatred, let me sow love;
Where there is injury, pardon;
Where there is doubt, faith;
Where there is despair, hope;
Where there is darkness, light;
Where there is sadness, joy.

O Divine Master, grant that I may not so much seek to be consoled as to console; to be understood as to understand; to be loved as to love.

For it is in giving that we receive; it is in pardoning that we are pardoned; and it is in dying that we are born to eternal life. Amen.

A Prayer to One's Own Patron Saint

O heavenly patron, in whose name I glory, pray ever to God for me; strengthen me in my faith; establish me in virtue; guard me in the conflict; that I may vanquish the foe malign and attain to glory everlasting. Amen.

Litany of the Saints

Lord, have mercy on us.

Christ, have mercy on us.

Lord, have mercy on us.

Christ, hear us.

Christ, graciously hear us.

God the Father of heaven, *have mercy on us.*

God the Son, Redeemer of the world, *have mercy on us.*

God the Holy Spirit, *have mercy on us.*

Holy Trinity, one God, *have mercy on us.*

Holy Mary, Mother of God, *[after each invocation, the response is:] pray for us.*

Holy angels of God,

St. Joseph,

St. John the Baptist,

St. Peter and St. Paul,

St. Andrew,

St. John,

St. Mary Magdalene,

St. Stephen,

St. Ignatius,

St. Lawrence,

St. Perpetua and St. Felicity,

St. Agnes,

St. Gregory,

St. Augustine,

St. Basil,

St. Martin,

St. Benedict,
St. Francis and St. Dominic,
St. Francis Xavier,
St. John Vianney,
St. Catherine,
St. Teresa,
St. Francis Xavier Cabrini,
St. Elizabeth Seton,
St. John Neumann,
All you holy men and women, saints of God, *make
    intercession for us.*
All you holy saints and blesseds of North and South
    America, *make intercession for us.*
Be merciful; *spare us, O Lord.*
Be merciful; *graciously hear us, O Lord.*
From all evil, *[after each invocation, the response is:]
    O Lord, deliver us.*
From all sin,
From your wrath,
From sudden and unprovided death,
From the snares of the devil,
From anger, hatred, and every evil will,
From the spirit of fornication,
From lightning and tempest,
From the scourge of earthquake,
From plague, famine, and death,
From everlasting death,
We sinners beseech you, *hear us.*

That you would spare us, *[after each invocation, the response is:] we beseech you, hear us.*
That you would pardon us,
That you would bring us to true penance,
That you would carefully govern and preserve your holy Church,
That you would carefully preserve our Holy Father and all orders of the Church, in holy religion,
That you would grant grace and true unity to all Christian people,
That you would graciously confirm and preserve us in your holy service,
That you would bring back all the erring to the unity of the Church, and lead all to the light of the Gospel,
That you would deliver our souls and the souls of our relatives, friends, and benefactors from eternal damnation,
That you would graciously give and preserve the fruits of the earth,
That you would distribute the goods of the earth with justice,
That you would graciously grant eternal life to all the faithful departed,
That you would graciously hear us,
Son of God,

Lamb of God, who take away the sins of the world, *spare us, O Lord.*

Lamb of God, who take away the sins of the world,
    graciously hear us, O Lord.
Lamb of God, who take away the sins of the world,
    have mercy on us.

Christ, *hear us.*
Christ, *graciously hear us.*
Lord, *have mercy.*
Christ, *have mercy.*
Lord, *have mercy.*

Let us pray: O heavenly Father, graciously hear our petitions and mercifully lead us on the way to eternal life. Inflame our hearts with the fire of the Holy Spirit, that each hour and each day may deepen our gratitude and love for you, so that we shall be faithful until death, through the merits of your divine Son, our Lord Jesus Christ. Amen.

A Prayer for the Faithful Departed

Eternal rest grant unto them, O Lord, and let perpetual light shine upon them. May their souls and the souls of all the faithful departed, through the mercy of God, rest in peace. Amen.

A Fatima Prayer

O my Jesus, forgive us our sins, save us from the power of hell and lead all souls to heaven, especially those most in need of your mercy. Amen.

Preface of the Dead

Father, all-powerful and ever-living God,
we do well always and everywhere to give you thanks
through Jesus Christ our Lord.

In him, who rose from the dead,
our hope of resurrection dawned.
The sadness of death gives way
to the bright promise of immortality.
Lord, for your faithful people life is changed, not
    ended.
When the body of our earthly dwelling lies in death
we gain an everlasting dwelling place in heaven.

And so, with all the choirs of angels in heaven
we proclaim your glory
and join in their unending hymn of praise:

Holy, holy, holy Lord, God of power and might,
heaven and earth are full of your glory.
Hosanna in the highest.
Blessed is he who comes in the name of the Lord.
Hosanna in the highest.

Prayers for the Dead

    • Lord Jesus, listen to our prayers for our
brother (sister) N., as he (she) always desired to do
your will, so in your mercy forgive whatever wrong
he (she) may have done. By his (her) Christian faith,
he (she) was united to your people. Now, in love and

mercy grant him (her) a place with your angels and
saints. We ask this through Christ our Lord. Amen.

• Father, God of all consolation, in your
unending love and mercy for us, you turn the
darkness of death into the dawn of a new life. Show
compassion to your people in their sorrow. Be our
refuge and our strength to lift us from the darkness
of this grief to the peace and light of your presence.
Your Son, our Lord Jesus Christ, by dying for us,
conquered death, and by rising again, restored life.
May we then go forward to meet him eagerly, and
after our life on earth be reunited with our brothers
and sisters where every tear will be wiped away. We
ask this through Christ our Lord. Amen.

• Dying you destroyed our death, rising you
restored our life; Lord Jesus, come in glory.

A Prayer of Robert Grant

O worship the king, all glorious above;
O gratefully sing his power and his love;
Our shield and defender, the ancient of days,
Pavilioned in splendor and girded with praise.

O tell of his might, O sing of his grace;
Whose robe is the light, whose canopy space;
His chariots of wrath the deep thunder clouds form,
And dark is his path on the wings of the storm.

This earth with its store of wonders untold,
Almighty, your power has founded of old;

Has 'stablished it fast by a changeless decree,
And round it has cast, like a mantle, the sea.

Your bountiful care what tongue can recite?
It breathes in the air, it shines in the night;
It streams from the hills, it descends to the plain,
And sweetly distills in the dew and the rain.

Frail children of dust, and feeble as frail,
In you do we trust, nor find you to fail;
Your mercies so tender, how firm to the end,
Our maker, defender, redeemer, and friend.

O measureless might, ineffable love,
While angels delight to hymn you above,
Your humbler creation, though feeble our lays,
With true adoration shall sing to your praise.

Prayer for Generosity
(Mary Stuart — Mary, Queen of Scots)
Keep me, O God, from pettiness.
Let us be large in thought, word, and deed.
Let us be done with fault-finding and leave off
self-seeking. May we put away all pretense and
meet each other face to face without self-pity
and without prejudice.

May we never be hasty in judgment and always
generous.

Let us take time for all things.
Make us grow calm, serene, gentle.

Teach us to put into action our better impulses, and
    make us straightforward and unafraid.

Grant that we may realize that it is the little things in
    life that create differences; that in the big things
    we are all one.
And, O Lord God,
Let us not forget to be kind. Amen.

PART 3

The Living Tradition—
Meditations and Readings

Writings of the Saints and Others

From 'The First Apology,' Chs. 32, 33
(St. Justin, Martyr)

The prophet Isaiah put it this way, "A star shall rise out of Jacob and a flower shall spring from the root of Jesse, and in his arm shall nations trust." Indeed, a brilliant star has arisen, and a flower has sprung up from the root of Jesse — this is Christ. For, by God's power He was conceived of a Virgin who was a descendant of Jacob, who was the father of Judah, the father of the Jewish race; and Jesse was his forefather according to this prophecy, and He was the son of Jacob and Judah according to his lineage.

Again, hear how it was expressly foretold by Isaiah that He was to be born of a Virgin. Here is the prophecy, "Behold, a virgin shall conceive and bear a son, and his name shall be called Emmanuel (God is with us!)." For what man has deemed incredible and impossible, God foretold through the prophetic spirit as about to take place, so that, when they take place, they should not be denied but believed because they have been predicted.

Let us attempt to explain the words of this prophecy. The words "Behold a virgin shall conceive" mean that the virgin shall conceive without intercourse. If she had had intercourse with anyone whomsoever, she was no longer a virgin, but the power of God descending upon the virgin overshadowed her and caused her, while still a virgin, to conceive.

And the angel of God who was then sent to that same virgin carried the glad news to her when he said, "Behold, you will conceive in your womb of the Holy Spirit, and you shall bring forth a Son and he shall be called the Son of the Most High, and you shall call his name Jesus, for he shall save his people from their sins."

This happened as related by those who recorded all the acts of our Savior, Jesus Christ, whom we believed, and through the above mentioned Isaiah, the prophetic spirit foretold that He would be born in the manner just stated. And it was the Holy Spirit who came upon the Virgin, overshadowed her, and brought it about that she became pregnant, not by sexual power but by divine power.

Jesus is a name in the Hebrew language which means Savior in the Greek; thus the angel said to the virgin, "And you shall name him Jesus for he shall save his people from their sins."

From 'Letters'
(St. Ignatius of Antioch)
Come together in common, one and all without exception in charity, in one faith and in one Lord,

Jesus Christ, who is of the race of David according to the flesh, the son of man and the Son of God, so that with undivided mind you may obey the bishop and the priests, and break one Bread which is the medicine of immortality and the antidote against death, enabling us to live forever in Jesus Christ.

Be zealous, then, in the observance of one Eucharist. For there is one Flesh of our Lord Jesus Christ, and one chalice that brings union in his Blood. There is one altar as there is one bishop with the priests and deacons, who are my fellow workers. And so, whatever you do, let it be done in the name of God.

Desire within me has been nailed to the cross and no flame of material longing is left. Only the living water speaks within me saying, "Hasten to the Father." I have no taste for the food that perishes nor for the pleasures of this life. I want the Bread of God which is the Flesh of Christ, and for drink I desire his Blood, which is love that cannot be destroyed.

For there is one Doctor who is active in both body and soul, begotten and yet unbegotten, God in man, true life in death, son of Mary and Son of God, first able to suffer and then unable to suffer, Jesus Christ our Lord.

And so, be deaf when anyone speaks to you apart from Jesus Christ, who was of the race of David, the son of Mary, who was truly born and ate and drank, who was truly persecuted under Pontius

Pilate and was really crucified and died in the sight of those "in heaven and on the earth and under the earth."

Moreover, he was truly raised from the dead by the power of the Father; in like manner his Father, through Jesus Christ, will raise up those of us who believe in him. Apart from him we have no true life.

From 'Letter to the Corinthians'
(St. Clement of Rome)

For Christ belongs to the humble-minded, not to those who exalt themselves over his flock. The scepter of the majesty of God, the Lord Jesus Christ, came not in the pomp of boasting or of arrogance, though he was mighty; but he was humble-minded as the Holy Spirit spoke concerning him.

For he says, "Lord, who has believed our report and to whom is the arm of the Lord revealed? We announced his presence: he is as a child, as a root in thirsty ground. There is no beauty in him, nor comeliness, and we have seen him and he had neither form nor beauty." You see, beloved, what is the example given us. If the Lord was thus humble-minded, what shall we do who through him have come under the yoke of his grace?

This is the way by which we found our Savior, Jesus Christ, the high priest of our offerings, the protector and helper of our weakness. Through him let us strain our eyes toward the heights of heaven;

through him we see mirrored his spotless and glorious countenance.

Through him the eyes of our hearts have been opened; through him our foolish and darkened understanding shoots up into light; through him the Lord willed that we should taste immortal knowledge. "Who, being the brightness of his Majesty, is so much greater than the angels as he has inherited a more excellent name."

In charity, then, the Lord received us; out of the charity which he had for us, Jesus Christ our Lord gave his Blood for us by the will of God, and his Flesh for our flesh, and his life for our lives.

Who can explain the bond of the charity of God? Who can express the splendor of its beauty? The height to which charity lifts us is inexpressible. Charity unites us to God. "Charity covers a multitude of sins." Charity bears all things and is long-suffering in all things.

There is nothing mean in charity, nothing arrogant. Charity knows no schism, does not rebel, does all things in peace and concord. In charity, all the elect of God have been made perfect. Without charity, nothing is pleasing to God.

From 'Letter to the Philippians'
(St. Polycarp)

Without interruption let us persevere by our hope and by the guarantee of our righteousness, which is Jesus Christ, who "bore our sins in his own body on the tree, who did no sin, nor was deceit found in his mouth"; but for our sake, that we might live in him, he endured all things.

Let us become imitators of his patient endurance, and, if we suffer for his name, let us praise him. He gave us this example in his own body and we have believed this.

Stand fast, therefore, in this conduct and follow the example of the Lord, "firm and unchangeable in faith, lovers of the brotherhood, loving each other, united in truth," helping each other with the mildness of the Lord, despising no one.

When you can do good, do not put it off, "for almsgiving frees from death." You must all be subject to one another and keep your conduct free from reproach among pagans so that from your good works you may receive praise and the Lord may not be blasphemed on your account. Teach sobriety to all, and practice it yourselves.

Now, may God and the Father of our Lord Jesus Christ and the eternal high priest himself, Jesus Christ, build you up in faith and truth and all kindness, free from anger, patient, long-suffering in endurance and chastity. May he give you a share and participation among his saints, and to us along with you, as well as to all under heaven who shall believe in our Lord and God, Jesus Christ, and in his Father who raised him up from the dead.

Pray for all the saints. Pray also for your rulers and even for those who persecute and hate you, and for all the enemies of the Cross, that the result of your effort may be manifest to all, and that you may be perfect in him.

From 'On the Unity of the Church'
(St. Cyprian)

Who is so profane and lacking in faith, who so insane by the fury of discord as either to believe that the unity of God, the garment of the Lord, the Church of Christ, can be torn asunder or to dare to do so? He himself tells us in his gospel, "There shall be one flock and one shepherd."

Does anyone think that there can be either many shepherds or many flocks in one place? The Apostle Paul teaches the same unity when he begs and urges us in these words, "I beseech you, brethren, by the name of our Lord Jesus Christ, that you may all say the same thing, and that there be no dissensions among you; but that you be perfectly united in the same mind and in the same judgment."

Again he says, "Bear with one another in love, careful to preserve the unity of the Spirit, in the bond of peace." Do you think you can stand and live, withdrawing from the Church, and building for yourself other abodes and different dwellings, when it was said to Rahab, in whom the Church was prefigured, "You shall gather your father and your

mother and your brethren and the entire house of
your father to your own self in your house, and it
will be that everyone who goes out of the door of
your house shall be his own accuser."

The flesh of Christ and the holy things of the
Lord cannot be carried outside, and there is no other
house for believers except the one Church. This
house, this hospice of unanimity the Holy Spirit
designates and proclaims when he says, "God makes
those of one mind who dwell in his house."

In the house of God, in the Church of Christ,
those of one mind dwell; they persevere in concord
and simplicity. This unanimity existed of old among
the Apostles, and the first assembly of believers
guarded the commandments of the Lord with charity.

"But the multitude of those who believed acted
with one soul and one mind." And again, "And all
were persevering with one mind in prayer with the
women and Mary the mother of Jesus and his
brethren." Thus they prayed with efficacious
prayers; thus they were able with confidence to
obtain whatever they asked of God's mercy.

From 'Letter to Emperor Leo'
(Pope St. Leo the Great)

What reconciliation could there be in which God
might again be made propitious to the human race if
the Mediator between God and man did not take
upon himself the cause of all men? How, indeed,

might anyone fulfill the reality of a mediator unless he shared in the nature of God, equal to the Father, and also in our servile nature, so that the bonds of death, brought about by the sin of Adam, might be loosed by the death of One who alone was in no way the subject of death?

The outpouring of Christ's blood for sinners was so rich in value that, if all the enslaved believed in their Redeemer, none of them would be held by the chains of the devil. For, as the Apostle says, "Where sin has abounded, grace has abounded yet more." And, since those born under the sentence of original sin have received the power of rebirth unto justification, the gift of freedom became stronger than the debt of slavery.

Consequently, what hope do they leave themselves in the refuge of this mystery who deny the reality of the human body of our Savior? Let them say by what sacrifice they have become reconciled. Let them say by what blood they have been redeemed.

Who is there, as the Apostle says, that "has delivered himself up for us an offering and a sacrifice to God to ascend in fragrant odor"? Or what sacrifice was ever more holy than that which the true and eternal Priest placed upon the altar of the cross by the immolation of his own flesh?

Although the death of many holy people was precious in the sight of the Lord, the redemption of the world was not effected by the killing of any of these guiltless persons. The just received crowns; they did not give them. From the courage of the faithful came examples of patience, not the gifts of justification. Indeed, their individual deaths affected them individually, but none gave his life to pay another's debts.

Among the sons of men only one stood out, our Lord Jesus Christ, who was truly the spotless Lamb, in whose person all were crucified, all died, all were buried, and all were raised from the dead.

From 'The Fourth Dialogue'
(Pope St. Gregory the Great)

In the Gospel, our Lord says, "Finish your journey while you still have the light." And in the words of the prophet he declares, "In an acceptable time I have heard you, and in the day of salvation I have helped you."

St. Paul's comment on this is, "And here in the time of pardon, the day of salvation has come already." Solomon says, "Anything you can turn your hand to, do with what power you have; for there will be no work, nor reason, nor knowledge, nor wisdom in the nether world where you are going." And David adds, "For his mercy endures forever."

From these quotations it is clear that each one will be presented to the Judge exactly as he was when he departed this life. Yet, there must be a cleansing fire before judgment because of some minor faults that may remain to be purged away.

Does not Christ the Truth say that if anyone blasphemes against the Holy Spirit he shall not be forgiven "either in this world or in the world to come"? From this statement we learn that some sins can be forgiven in this world and some in the world to come.

This must apply to slight transgressions, such as persistent idle gossip, immoderate laughter, or blame in the care of property, which can scarcely be administered without fault even by those who know the faults to be avoided, or errors due to ignorance in matters of no great import.

All these faults are troublesome for the soul after death if they are not forgiven while one is still alive. For, when St. Paul says that Christ is the foundation, he goes on to say, "But on this foundation different men will build in gold, silver, precious stones, wood, grass or straw . . . and fire will test the quality of each man's workmanship."

He will receive a reward if the building he has added on stands firm. If it is burnt up, he will be the loser; and yet he himself will be saved, though only as men are saved by passing through fire. This may signify the fire of suffering we experience in this life or the cleansing fire in the world to come.

From 'Confessions,' Bk. 27
(St. Augustine)

Late have I loved you, O Beauty ever ancient, ever new, late have I loved you! Behold, you were within and I was without. I was looking for you out there, and I threw myself, deformed as I was, upon those well-formed things which you had made.

You were with me, yet I was not with you. These things held me far from you, things which would not have existed had they not been in you. You called and cried out and burst in upon my deafness; you lighted up and glowed to drive away my blindness.

You sent forth your fragrance and I drew in my breath, and now I pant for you. I have tasted and now I hunger and thirst. You touched me and I was inflamed with the desire for your peace.

From 'The City of God,' Bk. 9
(St. Augustine)

But, if it be inevitable that all men, so long as they are mortal, must also be miserable — a contention far more credible and probable — then we must seek a Mediator who is not only human, but also divine in order that, by the intervention of his blessed mortality, men may be led from their mortal misery to a blessed immortality. It was necessary for the mediator to become, but not remain, mortal.

Indeed, he became incarnate not by any

diminution of the divinity of the Word, but by assuming the frailty of flesh. The very fruit of his mediation is precisely this: that they for whose liberation he became a mediator should not remain forever subject even to the death of the flesh.

The mediator between God and man was to possess a passing mortality and an enduring beatitude, so that, by means of passing elements, he might be conformed to men who are mortal and then transport them from death to that which endures. Therefore, the good angels cannot be mediators between miserable mortals and happy immortals because they, also, are both blessed and immortal.

The good Mediator was willing to become mortal for a time though able to remain blessed for eternity. He, by the humility of his death and the benignity of his beatitude, has destroyed the diabolic reign in those whose hearts he cleansed by faith and liberation.

However, the fact that Christ is the Word is not the reason why he became the Mediator; for certainly, the Word at the summit of immortality and the apex of beatitude is far removed from miserable mortals. Rather, he is the Mediator because he is man, and as man shows us that to attain the Supreme Good, blessed and beatific, we need not seek other mediators to serve as rungs on a ladder of ascent.

For the blessed God who makes us blessed, by deigning to share our humanity, showed us the

shortest way to sharing his divinity. Freeing us from
mortality and misery he leads us directly to that
Trinity in communion with which even the angels are
blessed.

From 'Confessions,' Bk. 9
(St. Augustine)

The day was now approaching when my
mother, Monica, would depart from this life; you
knew that day, Lord, though we did not. She and I
happened to be standing by ourselves at a window
overlooking the garden in the courtyard of the house.

At that time we were in Ostia on the Tiber. We
had gone there after a long and wearisome journey to
get away from the noisy crowd, and to rest and to
prepare for our sea voyage. I believe, Lord, that you
caused all this to happen in your own mysterious
ways.

And so the two of us, all alone, were enjoying a
very pleasant conversation, forgetting the past and
pushing on to what is ahead. We were asking one
another in the presence of the Truth — for you are
the Truth — what it would be like to share eternal life
such as that enjoyed by the saints, which "eye has
not seen, nor ear heard, nor has it even entered into
the heart of man." We desired with all our hearts to
drink from the streams of your heavenly fountain,
the fountain of life.

That was the substance of our talk, though not

the exact words. But you know, O Lord, that in the course of our conversation that day, the world and its pleasures lost all their attraction for us.

My mother said, "Son, as far as I am concerned, nothing in this life now gives me any pleasure. I do not know why I am still here, since I have no further hopes in this world. I did have one reason to want to live a little longer: to see you become a Christian before I die. God has lavished his gifts on me in this respect, for I know that you have even renounced earthly happiness to be his servant."

I do not really remember how I replied to her. Shortly, within about five days, she fell sick with a fever. Then one day during the course of her illness she became unconscious and for a time she was unaware of her surroundings.

My brother and I rushed to her side but she regained consciousness quickly. She looked at us as we stood there and asked in a puzzled voice, "Where was I?" We remained overwhelmed with grief but she spoke further, "Here you shall bury your mother."

I remained silent as I held back my tears. However, my brother haltingly expressed his hope that she wouldn't die in a foreign land, but in her own country, since her end would be happier there. When she heard this her face filled with anxiety and she reproached him with a glance.

Then she said to both of us, "Bury my body

wherever you will, let not care of it cause you any concern. One thing only I ask you, that you remember me at the altar of the Lord wherever you may be."

From 'Missus Est,' Homilies I
(St. Bernard of Clairvaux — the Last of the Fathers, and the Troubadour of Mary)

Gabriel was not, in my opinion, an angel of one of the lowest orders who are so often sent into the world on various matters. I take this from his name which means "Strength of God" and from the fact that he was a direct emissary from God and not from some higher-ranking angel, as might have happened. Perhaps this is the reason the Gospel adds "from God," or it could be to show that God did not reveal his plan to anyone before the Virgin, except the archangel Gabriel.

Only Gabriel was found worthy among the archangels of the name and the message, between which there is real harmony. Who could better announce the power of God, Christ, than an angel bearing that name? Is not power strength? It is hardly incongruous that our Lord and his messenger should be designated by the same word. However, what is similar in word is not necessarily similar in origin! Christ is essentially the power, or strength of God. For the angel it is only a name.

Christ is called, and is, the Power of God. He is that conquering hero who overcomes the stronghold of the armed man, and who, by his strength, liberates captives.

The angel is called the strength of God either as a prerogative of his office, announcing the advent of the Power of God, or because it was his privilege to strengthen the Virgin so that this unique miracle would not frighten her in her natural humility and simplicity. He certainly did strengthen her when he said, "Do not be afraid, Mary, because you have found grace before God."

It was fitting that Gabriel be chosen for such a work; indeed, because he was to be engaged in so great a mission, it was fitting that so great a name be given him.

* * *

Mary calls him "Son" who is the God and Lord of the angels, saying, "Son, why have you done this to us?" What angel would dare say that! They consider it a rare privilege, being spirits, simply to be his messengers and do his bidding. As David affirms, "He has created angels to be his messengers."

Mary, recognizing her position as his Mother, did not hesitate to call him "Son" whom the angels serve in reverence. Nor did God hesitate to respond to the name and to revere the maternal majesty he had bestowed on her.

A little further on, the Evangelist says, "And he

went down to Nazareth and was subject to them."
Who was subject to whom? God was subject to man!
The God who commands all the orders of angels was
subject to Mary.

Which shall we admire first? The tremendous
submission of the Son of God, or the tremendous
God-given dignity of the Mother of God? Both are
amazing; both are marvels.

When God obeys a woman, it is humility
without precedent. When a woman commands her
God, it is sublime above measure. In praising virgins
we read that they follow the Lamb wherever he goes.
How can we possibly praise sufficiently the Virgin
who leads him?

Learn, O man, to obey; learn, O earth, to be
subject; learn, O dust, to bow down. In speaking of
your creator the Evangelist says, "He was subject to
them." Blush, proud ashes, for God humiliates
himself and you exalt yourself. God submits to men,
but you, ignoring his example, seek to dominate your
fellow men.

O Blessed Virgin Mary! You lacked neither
humility nor virginity. And it is a truly remarkable
virginity which did not fear, but rather honored,
fruitfulness.

We certainly should not be surprised that God,
who is blessed and wonderful in his saints, should be
yet more marvelous in his Mother. Virgins may
praise the motherhood of this Virgin; the married

may honor the virginity of this Mother. All can
imitate the humility of the Mother of God.

From 'Missus Est,' Homilies II
(St. Bernard)

"And the Virgin's name was Mary." Let us say a
few things about this name, which can be interpreted
to mean "Star of the Sea," an apt designation for the
Virgin Mother.

She is most beautifully likened to a star, for a
star pours forth its light without losing anything of
its nature. She gave us her Son without losing
anything of her virginity. The glowing rays of a star
take nothing away from its beauty. Neither has the
Son taken anything away from his Mother's
integrity.

She is that noble star of Jacob, illuminating the
whole world, penetrating from the highest heavens to
the deepest depths of hell. The warmth of her
brilliance shines in the minds of men, encouraging
virtue, extinguishing vice. She is that glorious star
lighting the way across the vast ocean of life, glowing
with merits, guiding by example.

When you find yourself tossed by the raging
storms on this great sea of life, far from land, keep
your eyes fixed on this Star to avoid disaster. When
the winds of temptation or the rocks of tribulation
threaten, look up to the Star, call upon Mary.

When the waves of pride or ambition sweep

over you, when the tide of detraction or jealousy runs against you, look up to the Star, call upon Mary! When the shipwreck of avarice, anger, or lust seems imminent, call upon Mary!

If the horror of sin overwhelms you and the voice of conscience terrifies you, if the fear of judgment, the abyss of sadness, and the depths of despair clutch at your heart, think of Mary! In dangers, difficulties, and doubts, think about Mary, call upon Mary!

Keep her name on your lips, her love in your heart. Imitate her, and her powerful intercession will surround you. Following her, you will not stray. Praying to her, you will ward off disaster and despair. Meditate about her and you will not err. Cling to her and you cannot fall.

With her protection, there is nothing to fear. Under her leadership you will succeed. With her encouragement, all is possible.

From 'Treatise on the Love of God,' Ch. 1
(St. Bernard)

Do you wish to hear from me why and how God should be loved? The reason for loving God is God himself. The way to love him is beyond measure.

Is this enough? It is for one who is wise. But if to the unwise I am a debtor, where enough has been said to the wise, I must also, as usual, administer to the needs of others. Out of consideration for those who are slower in understanding, I consider it no burden to repeat what I have said, more fully if not more profoundly.

There is a twofold reason why God should be loved for his own sake: because nothing can be more justly, or more profitably, loved. When the question is asked why God should be loved, it may have two meanings. The question may arise from the fact that a person does not clearly see what particularly constitutes the basis of his inquiry — whether it is God's title to our love or to our own advantage in loving him.

I would give the same answer to both questions. I find no other worthy reason for loving him, except himself. The special title that God has to our love is that it is he who gave himself to us despite the fact that we are so undeserving. It is then, chiefly, that God has first loved us. He clearly deserves to be loved in return if one considers who he is that loved, who they are whom he loved, and how much he loved them.

Who is he? He is the One to whom every good spirit testifies, "You are my God; you have no need of my goods." And the true love of this sovereign One lies in this, that he does not seek his own interests.

But to whom is such unalloyed love shown? "When we were his enemies we were reconciled to God." God has loved his enemies, and that freely.

And how much? St. John testifies, "God so loved the world that he gave his only-begotten Son." St. Paul adds, "He spared not even his own Son but delivered him up for all of us."

That very Son says to himself, "Greater love than this no one has, that one lay down his life for his friends." Thus has the just One deserved from the ungodly, the Greatest from the least, the Omnipotent from the weak.

'Is Mary the Mother of God?'
From 'Summa Theologica,'
Bk. 3, Q. 35, Art. 4
(St. Thomas Aquinas)

It would seem that the Blessed Virgin should not be called the Mother of God. In things divine we should not assert what cannot be found in Holy Scripture, and nowhere do we see the title Mother or Parent of God, only Mother of Christ, or Mother of the Infant.

Furthermore, Christ is called God according to the divine nature. The divine nature did not begin to be because of this Virgin, so we should not call her the Mother of God.

And even more serious: the word "God" is regularly used for the Father, the Son and the Holy Spirit. If the Blessed Virgin Mary is the Mother of God, it would seem to follow logically that she is the mother of the Father, as well as of the Son and of the

Holy Spirit. That is not true, so she should not be called the Mother of God in any way.

But on the contrary: In the works of St. Cyril as fully approved by the ecumenical Council of Ephesus, we read, "If anyone does not profess that Emmanuel is truly God, and that for this reason the Holy Virgin is the Mother of God, since she gave birth of her own flesh to the Word of God made flesh, let him be anathema."

My reply is that every word that signifies in the concrete can stand for any person having that nature. Since the union which took place is a personal (hypostatic) union, as proved previously, it is obvious that this word "God" can stand for a Person having a human and a divine nature.

Whatever belongs to the divine nature and whatever belongs to the human nature can be attributed to the Person. When a word is used to signify something belonging to the divine nature, or when a word is used to signify something belonging to the human nature, it can be attributed to the Person.

To be conceived and to be born are attributed to the Person (the Hypostasis) according to the nature conceived and born. Since the human nature was taken by the divine Person in the very instant of conception, it follows that it can be said in actual truth, that God was conceived and born of this Virgin. From this, a woman is called a man's mother, namely that she conceived him and gave him birth.

Therefore, the Blessed Virgin Mary is truly called the Mother of God.

The only way it could be denied that Mary is the Mother of God is if the humanity itself were the first subject of conception and birth before this man was the Son of God (cf. the heresy of Photinus); or if the humanity were not assumed into unity of Person (the Hypostasis) of the Word of God (cf. the heresy of Nestorius).

Both of these errors have been formally condemned. Therefore, it is heresy to deny that the Blessed Virgin Mary is the Mother of God.

My answers to the three objections stated above:

1. This objection was used by Nestorious, but it is easily solved by saying that even though we do not find it explicitly stated in Holy Scripture that Mary is the Mother of God, we do find it explicitly stated that the Blessed Virgin is the Mother of Jesus (Mt. 1:18) and that Jesus Christ is true God (1 Jn. 5:20). Therefore it necessarily follows that Mary is the Mother of God.

Furthermore, we read in Romans 9 that "Christ came from the Jews according to the flesh, who is above all, God blessed forever." The only way he came from the Jews is through the Blessed Virgin. Therefore he who is above all things and is God, blessed forever, is truly born of the Blessed Virgin as his Mother.

2. This was another objection of Nestorius.
Cyril writes about it, "Just as when a man's soul is
born with its own body, they are considered one
being, and, should anyone want to say that the
mother of the flesh is not also the mother of the soul,
he would be saying too much.

"We perceive something very much like this in
the generation of Christ. The Word of God was born
of the substance of the Father, but because he took
flesh, we must necessarily confess that he was born
in the flesh from a woman. Therefore we are obliged
to say that the Blessed Virgin is the Mother of God,
not that she is the Mother of Divinity, but because
she is the Mother, according to his human nature, of
the Person who has both the divine and the human
nature."

3. The name "God" is common to all three
Persons, but it is sometimes used for the Person of
the Father alone, sometimes for the Person of the Son
alone, and sometimes for the Person of the Holy
Spirit alone. We have proved this previously. When
we profess that the Blessed Virgin Mary is the
Mother of God, we acknowledge that she is the
Mother of the Incarnate Son of God.

'St. Thomas Aquinas — An Appreciation' From 'The Thirteenth, Greatest of Centuries' *(James J. Walsh)*

The appreciation of St. Thomas in his own time is the greatest tribute to the critical faculty of the century that could be made. So great was this appreciation that it almost made it too difficult for him to complete his work. Everyone wanted to hear him. Universities demanded his presence.

He was noted for the kindliness of his disposition and for his power to make friends. Looked upon as the greatest thinker of his time it would be easy to expect that there should be some consciousness of this. Thomas, however, never seems to have had any over-appreciation of his own talents, but realizing how little he knew compared to the whole round of knowledge, and how superficial his thinking was compared to the depth of the mysteries he was trying to treat, it must be admitted that there was no question of conceit in his life.

Thomas was the friend of the great minds of his age, and he was sought after by Popes and scholars. Pope Clement IV actually issued a bull making St. Thomas the Archbishop of Naples, but Thomas respectfully declined it. After this he worked on, and almost completed, the great work of his life, the *Summa.* Thomas sincerely and whole-heartedly pursued sanctity as the only real goal of human life.

From 'Imitation of Christ,' Bk. II, Ch. 11
(Thomas à Kempis)

Jesus has many followers who love his heavenly kingdom, but very few who carry the cross with him. There are many who want to share his consolations, but few his tribulations. Many companions join him at table, but few in fast and abstinence.

They all desire to rejoice with him, but few are willing to endure anything for his sake. Many follow Jesus to the breaking of bread, but few join him in drinking the cup of his passion. Many reverence his miracles, but few follow him on the way to the cross.

Many love Jesus as long as they meet no adversity; many praise him and bless him as long as they receive spiritual consolation from him.

But if Jesus hides himself and leaves them even for a little while, they either murmur or fall into dejection, excessively.

Those who love Jesus for his own sake, and not for the sake of their own consolation, bless him no less in trials and troubles than in the greatest consolation.

And if he should never give them consolation, yet they would always praise him and give him thanks. O how much this true love of Jesus is able to do when it is not mixed up in self-interest or self-love!

From 'Imitation of Christ,' Bk. II, Ch. 12
(Thomas à Kempis)

To many, this seems a very hard saying, "Deny yourself, take up your cross and follow Jesus." But it will be much harder to hear that last word, "Depart from me, you accursed, into everlasting fire."

For those who love to hear and follow the word of the cross shall not then fear the sentence of eternal condemnation. This sign of the cross shall be in the heavens when the Lord comes in judgment.

Then all the servants of the cross who in their lifetime have conformed themselves to him who was crucified shall come to Christ their judge with great confidence.

Why are you afraid to take up your cross which leads to the kingdom? In the cross is salvation; in the cross is life; in the cross is protection from enemies.

In the cross is infusion of heavenly sweetness; in the cross is strength of mind; in the cross is joy of spirit. In the cross is height of virtue; in the cross is the perfection of sanctity. There is no health of soul, nor hope of eternal life, but in the cross.

Therefore, take up your cross and follow Jesus and you shall go into life eternal. He has gone before you, carrying his cross, and he died for you on the cross so that you could carry your cross and long to die on it.

Because, if you die with him, you shall also live with him; if you are his companion in suffering, you shall also be his companion in glory. There is no better way to life and to true interior peace than the way of the holy cross and of daily mortification.

Go where you will, seek what you will and you shall not find a higher way above nor a safer way below, than the way of the holy cross.

Dispose all things according to your own will and as seems best for you, and you will still find something to suffer either willingly or unwillingly, and so you will always find the cross. It may be bodily pain or spiritual trials, there is always a cross to carry. . . .

If you carry the cross willingly, it will carry you and bring you to the place where there is no suffering. If you carry it unwillingly, you make it a heavier burden for yourself, and you must still carry it.

If you fling away one cross, without doubt you will find another, and perhaps a heavier cross.

Do not seek another way rather than this royal way, which is the way of the cross.

From 'Imitation of Christ,' Bk. IV, Ch. 1
(Thomas à Kempis)

Come to me, all you who labor and are burdened and I will refresh you (Matt. 11:28). The bread that I will give for the life of the world is my flesh (Jn. 6:51). Take and eat, this is my body which is being given for you. Do this in memory of me (Matt.

26:26). He who eats my flesh and drinks my blood abides in me and I in him (Jn. 6:56). These words which I have addressed to you are spirit and life (Jn. 6:63).

Lord Jesus Christ, eternal Truth, you have spoken these words at various times in your life. Since they are yours, and they are true, they ought to be received with gratitude. Since they are yours, they have become mine because you delivered them for my salvation.

These are words of tenderness, full of love. Only my sins keep me from responding to them fully. But you command that I approach with confidence, if I would be part of you. "Come," you say, "all you who labor and are heavily burdened, and I will refresh you."

What loving words for a sinner to hear. You invite the poor and needy to receive the Communion of your most holy Body! Who am I, Lord, that I would dare to approach you? The heaven of heavens cannot contain you, and you say, "Come to me."

From 'Introduction to the Devout Life,' Ch. III
(St. Francis de Sales)

During the time of creation, God commanded the plants to bring forth their fruits, each one after its own kind. So does he command all Christians, who are the living plants of his Church, to bring forth the fruits of their devotion, each according to his own character and vocation.

Devotion must be exercised in different ways by the gentleman, the working man, the servant, the prince, the widow, the maid, and the married. Not only this, but the practice of devotion must be also adapted to the strength, the employment, and the duties of each one in particular.

Is it fit that a Bishop should lead the solitary life of the Carthusian, or that married people should lay up no greater store of worldly goods than the Capuchin? If a tradesman were to spend the whole day in Church, like a member of a religious order, or were a religious continually exposed to encounter difficulties in the service of his neighbor as a Bishop is, would not such devotion be ridiculous, disorganized, and insupportable?

Nevertheless this fault is very common. Thus the world, which does not distinguish, or does not wish to distinguish, between real devotion and the indiscretion of those who imagine themselves to be devout, murmurs at devotion and censures it, as if it were unable to prevent these disorders.

No, true devotion does no harm whatever, but rather it gives perfection to all things. When it goes contrary to our lawful vocation, then, without doubt, it is false. As Aristotle said, "The bee extracts honey from flowers without injuring them," and leaves them as whole and as fresh as it found them.

True devotion does still better. It not only does no injury to any vocation to work, but on the contrary it adorns and beautifies them. Each vocation becomes more agreeable when united with devotion. The care of the family becomes more peaceful, the love of husband and wife more sincere, the service to the prince more faithful, and every type of employment more pleasant and agreeable.

Wheresoever we are, we can and should aspire to a perfect spiritual life.

From the Sermon 'On Loving Jesus'
(St. Alphonsus de Liguori)

All holiness, all perfection lies in our love for Jesus Christ our God, who is our Redeemer and our supreme Good. It is part of the love of God to acquire and nurture all the virtues which make a man perfect.

Has not God won for himself a claim on all our love? From all eternity he has loved us and it is in this vein that he speaks to us, "O man, consider carefully that I have first loved you. You had not yet appeared in the light of day, nor did the world exist, but already I loved you."

God knew that man is enticed by favors, so he bound him to his love by means of his gifts. All the gifts which he gave man were given to this end. He gave him a soul, made in his own likeness, and endowed with memory, intellect, and will; he gave him a body equipped with senses; it was for him that he created heaven and earth and such a variety of things.

He went further and bestowed on man the gift of himself. The eternal Father went so far as to give his only Son to make reparation for us and to call us back to a sinless life. In his Son he bestowed on us every good: grace, love, and heaven.

From 'Christ the Life of the Soul,' Ch. 1
(Abbot Columba Marmion)

"God chose us in Christ before the world began to be holy and blameless in his sight, to be full of love; he likewise predestined us through Christ Jesus to be his adopted sons — such was his will and pleasure — that all might praise the glorious favor he has bestowed on us in his beloved" (Eph. 1:4-6).

These are the terms in which the divine plan is set forth by the Apostle St. Paul, who had been caught up to the third heaven, and was chosen by God to bring to light, as he himself says, the economy of the mystery which has been hidden from all eternity in God.

We see the great Apostle laboring unceasingly to make known this eternal plan, established by God himself for the sanctification of our souls. God, who is the author of our salvation and the first source of our sanctity, could alone have made known to us what he desires of us in order that we may attain to him.

It is therefore extremely important to run in the race not as at an uncertainty, as one beating the air, but so as to obtain the prize; to know as perfectly as possible the divine idea of holiness; to examine it with the greatest care, so as to adapt ourselves to it, the plan traced out by God himself whereby we may attain to him. It is only at this price that our salvation and sanctification can be realized.

In so important a matter, in so vital a question, we must look at and weigh things as God looks at and weighs them. God judges all things in the light, and his judgment is the test of all truth. "We must not judge things according to our own liking," says St. Francis de Sales, "but according to that of God; this is the great secret. If we are holy according to our own will, we shall never be truly holy; we must be so according to God's will.

Divine wisdom is infinitely above human wisdom; God's thoughts contain possibilities of fruitfulness such as no created thought possesses. That is why God's plan is so wise that it cannot fail to reach its end because of any intrinsic insufficiency, but only through our own fault. If we leave the divine idea full freedom to operate in us, if we adapt ourselves to it with love and fidelity, it becomes extremely fruitful and may lead us to the most sublime sanctity.

And now God, not in order to add to his plenitude, but by it to enrich other beings, extends, as it were, his Paternity. God decrees to call creatures to share this divine life, so transcendent that God alone has the right to live by it, the eternal life communicated by the Father to the Only Son, and by them to the Holy Spirit.

In a transport of love which has its source in the fulness of Being and Good that God is, this life overflows from the bosom of divinity to reach and beatify beings drawn out of nothingness, by lifting them above their nature.

To these mere creatures God will give the condition and sweet name of children. By nature God has only one Son; by love he wills to have an innumerable multitude: that is *the grace of supernatural adoption.*

Hence, all holiness is to consist in this: to receive the divine life from Christ and by Christ, who possesses its fulness and who has been constituted the one Mediator; to keep this divine life and increase it unceasingly by an ever more perfect adhesion, an even closer union with him who is its source.

From 'Christ in His Mysteries,' Ch. XVII, Sect. 4
(Abbot Columba Marmion)

The Holy Spirit came for us. Those assembled in the Cenacle on the first Pentecost represented the whole Church. The Spirit comes that he may abide

with her forever. This is Christ's own promise: He
will dwell with you forever.

The Holy Spirit descended visibly upon the
Apostles at Pentecost; from that day, Holy Church
has been spreading over all the earth. She is the
kingdom of Jesus, and it is the Holy Spirit who, with
the Father and the Son, governs his kingdom. He
completes in souls the work of holiness begun by the
redemption. He is, in the Church, what the soul is to
the body: the Spirit that animates and quickens it,
the Spirit that safeguards unity, while his action
produces manifold and diverse effects. He brings all
her vigor and beauty.

See what abundance of grace and charismata
inundate the Church on Pentecost. We read in Acts,
the book which is the history of the beginning of the
Church, that the Holy Spirit came down visibly upon
those who were baptized and that he filled them with
marvellous graces. With what complacency St. Paul
enumerates them: Now there are varieties of gifts,
but the same Spirit who works all things in all. Now
the manifestation of the Spirit is given to everyone
for profit.

"To one through the Spirit is given the power to
speak wisdom and to another the power to speak
knowledge, according to the same Spirit; to another
the gift of healing in the one Spirit; to another the
working of miracles, to another prophecy; to another
the distinguishing of spirits; to another various kinds

of tongues." And the Apostle adds, "But all these things are the work of the one and same Spirit, who gives to each according as he will."

Since the Holy Spirit abides in the Church in a permanent indefectible manner, he exercises an unceasing action of life and sanctification. He renders her infallible in truth. By his action a wonderful supernatural fruitfulness springs up in the Church. He plants and unfolds in virgins, martyrs, and confessors those heroic virtues which are among the marks of holiness.

In a word, he is the Spirit who, by his inspirations, works in souls, rendering the Church, which Jesus acquired for himself by his most precious Blood, holy and without blemish, worthy of being presented by Christ to his Father, on the day of final triumph.

From 'The Idea of the University,' Ch. III
(Cardinal John Henry Newman)

Truth is the object of knowledge of whatever kind; and when we inquire what is meant by truth, I suppose it is right to answer that truth means facts and their relations, which stand towards each other pretty much as subjects and predicates in logic.

All that exists, as contemplated by the human mind, forms one large system or complex fact, and this of course resolves itself into an indefinite number of particular facts, which, as being portions

of the whole, have countless relations of every kind,
one towards another.

Knowledge is the apprehension of these facts,
whether in themselves, or in their mutual positions
and bearings. And, as all taken together form one
integral subject for contemplation, so there are no
natural or real limits between part and part; one is
ever running into another; all, as viewed by the
mind, are combined together, and possess a
correlative character one with another, from the
internal mysteries of the Divine Essence down to our
own sensations and consciousness, from the most
solemn appointments of the Lord of all down to what
may be called the accident of the hour, from the most
glorious seraph down to the vilest . . . of reptiles.

Now, it is not wonderful that with all its
capabilities, the human mind cannot take in this
whole vast fact as a single glance, or gain possession
of it at once. Like a short-sighted reader, its eyes pore
closely, and travel slowly, over the awful volume
which lies open for its inspection.

Or again, as we deal with some huge structure of
many parts and sides, the mind goes round about it,
noting down, first one thing, then another, as it best
may, and viewing it under different aspects, by way
of making progress towards mastering the whole. So
by degrees and by circuitous advances does it rise
aloft and subject to itself a knowledge of that
universe into which it has been born.

These various partial views or abstractions, by means of which the mind looks out upon its objects, are called sciences, and embrace respectively larger or smaller portions of the field of knowledge; sometimes extending far and wide, but superficially, sometimes with exactness over particular departments, sometimes occupied together on one and the same portion, sometimes holding one part in common, and then ranging on this side or that in absolute divergence from one another.

From the Sermon 'The Second Spring'
(Cardinal John Henry Newman)

We should judge rightly in our curiosity about a phenomenon like this: it must be a portentous event, and it is. It is an innovation, a miracle, I may say, in the course of human events.

The physical world revolves year by year and begins anew; but the political order of things does not renew itself, does not return; it continues, but it proceeds; there is no retrogression. This is so well understood by men of the day, that with them progress is idolized as another name for good.

The past never returns — it is never good — if we are to escape existing ills, it must be by going forward. The past is out of date; the past is dead. As well may the dead live to us, well may the dead profit us, as the past returns.

This, then, is the cause of this national

transport, this national cry which encompasses us. The past *has* returned, the dead lives. Thrones are overturned and never restored. States live and die, and then are matter only for history. Babylon was great, and Tyre, and Egypt, and Nineve, and shall never be great again.

The English Church was, and the English Church was not, and the English Church is once again. This is the portent, worthy of a cry. It is the coming in of a Second Spring; it is a restoration in the moral order such as that which yearly takes place in the physical.

Three centuries ago, and the Catholic Church, that great creation of God's power, stood in this land in pride of place. It had the honors of nearly a thousand years upon it; it was enthroned on some twenty Sees up and down the broad country; it was based on the will of a faithful people; it energized through ten thousand instruments of power and influence, and it was ennobled by a host of saints and martyrs. . . .

No one would have prophesied its fall, but still less would anyone have ventured to prophesy its rise again.

'The Hound of Heaven'
(Francis Thompson)
I fled Him, down the nights and down the days;
  I fled Him, down the arches of the years;

I fled Him, down the labyrinthine ways
  Of my own mind: and in the midst of tears
I hid from Him, and under running laughter.
      Up vistaed hopes I sped;
      And shot, precipitated,
  Adown Titanic glooms of chasmèd fears,
From those strong feet that followed, followed after
      that.
      But with unhurrying chase,
      And unperturbèd pace,
  Deliberate speed, majestic instancy,
      They beat — and a Voice beat
      More instant than the Feet —
"All things betray thee, who betrayest Me."

      I pleaded, outlaw-wise,
By many a hearted casement, curtained red,
  Trellised and intertwining charities;
(For, though I knew His love Who followèd,
      Yet was I sore adread
Lest, having Him, I must have naught beside).
  But, if one little casement parted wide,
  The gust of His approach would clash it to.
  Fear wist not to evade, as Love wist to pursue.
Across the margent of the world I fled,
  And troubled the gold gateways of the stars,
  Smiting for shelter on their clangèd bars;
      Fretted to dulcet jars
And silver chatter the pale ports o' the moon.

I said to Dawn: Be sudden — to Eve: Be soon;
  With thy young skiey blossoms heap me over
    From this tremendous Lover —
Float thy vague veil about me, lest He see!
  I tempted all His servitors, but to find
My own betrayal in their constancy,
In faith to Him their fickleness to me,
  Their traitorous trueness, and their loyal deceit.
To all swift things for swiftness did I sue;
  Clung to the whistling mane of every wind.
    But whether they swept, smoothly fleet,
    The long savannahs of the blue;
      Or whether, Thunder-driven,
      They clanged his chariot 'thwart a heaven
Plashy with flying lightnings round the spurn o'
      their feet: —
  Fear wist not to evade as Love wist to pursue.
      Still with unhurrying chase,
      And unperturbèd pace,
    Deliberate speed, majestic instancy,
      Came on the following Feet,
      And a Voice above their beat —
    "Naught shelters thee, who wilt not shelter
      Me."
I sought no more that after which I strayed
    In face of man or maid;
But still within the little children's eyes
    Seems something, something that replies;
They at least are for me, surely for me!

I turned me to them very wistfully;
But, just as their young eyes grew sudden fair
   With dawning answers there,
Their angel plucked them from me by the hair.
"Come then, ye other children, Nature's — share
With me" (said I) "your delicate fellowship;
     Let me greet you lip to lip,
     Let me twine with you caresses,
       Wantoning
     With our Lady-Mother's vagrant tresses,
       Banqueting
     With her in her wind-walled palace,
     Underneath her azured daïs,
     Quaffing, as your taintless way is,
       From a chalice
Lucent-weeping out of the dayspring."
       So it was done:
I in their delicate fellowship was one —
Drew the bolt of Nature's secrecies.
     I knew all the swift importings
     On the wilful face of skies;
     I knew how the clouds arise
     Spumèd of the wild sea-snortings;
       All that's born or dies
     Rose and drooped with; made them shapers
Of mine own moods, or wailful or divine;
     With them joyed and was bereaven.
     I was heavy with the even,
     When she lit her glimmering tapers

Round the day's dead sanctities,
    I laughed in the morning's eyes.
I triumphed and I saddened with all weather,
    Heaven and I wept together,
And its sweet tears were salt with mortal mine;
Against the red throb of its sunset-heart
    I laid my own to beat,
    And share commingling heat;
But not by that, by that, was eased my human smart.
In vain my tears were wet on Heaven's grey cheek.
For ah! we know not what each other says,
   These things and I; in sound *I* speak —
Their sound is but their stir, they speak by silences.
Nature, poor stepdame, cannot slake my drought;
   Let her, if she would owe me,
Drop you blue bosom-veil of sky, and show me
   The breasts o' her tenderness:
Never did any milk of hers once bless
    My thirsting mouth.
    Nigh and nigh draws the chase,
    With unperturbèd pace,
  Deliberate speed, majestic instancy;
    And past those noisèd feet
    A Voice comes yet more fleet —
"Lo! naught contents thee, who content'st not Me."

Naked I wait Thy Love's uplifted stroke!
My harness piece by piece Thou hast hewn from me,
    And smitten me to my knee;

I am defenceless utterly.
I slept, methinks, and woke,
And, slowly gazing, find me stripped in sleep.
In the rash lustihead of my young powers,
I shook the pillaring hours
And pulled my life upon me; grimed with smears,
I stand amid the dust o' the mounded years —
My mangled youth lies dead beneath the heap.
My days have crackled and gone up in smoke,
Have puffed and burst as sun-starts on a stream.
Yea, faileth now even dream
The dreamer, and the lute the lutanist;
Even the linked fantasies, in whose blossomy twist
I swung the earth a trinket at my wrist,
Are yielding; cords of all too weak account
For earth with heavy griefs so overplussed.
Ah! is Thy love indeed
A weed, albeit an amaranthine weed,
Suffering no flowers except its own to mount?
Ah! must —
Designer infinite! —
Ah! must Thou char the wood ere Thou canst limn
with it?
My freshness spent its wavering shower i' the dust;
And now my heart is as a broken fount
Wherein tear-drippings stagnate, spilt down ever
From the dank thoughts that shiver
Upon the sighful branches of my mind.
Such is; what is to be?

The pulp so bitter, how shall taste the rind?
I dimly guess what Time in mists confounds;
Yet ever and anon a trumpet sounds
From the hid battlements of Eternity;
Those shaken mists a space unsettle, then
Round the half-glimpsèd turrets slowly wash again.
   But not ere him who summoneth
   I first have seen, enwound
With glooming robes purpureal, cypress-crowned;
His name I know, and what his trumpet saith.
Whether man's heart or life it be which yields
   Thee harvest, must Thy harvest-fields
   Be dunged with rotten death?

   Now of that long pursuit
   Comes on at hand the bruit;
That Voice is round me like a bursting sea:
      "And is thy earth so marred,
      Shattered in shard on shard?
   Lo! all things fly thee, for thou fliest Me!
   Strange, piteous, futile thing!
Wherefore should any set thee love apart?
Seeing none but I makes much of naught" (He said),
"And human love needs human meriting:
   How hast thou merited —
Of all man's clotted clay the dingiest clot?
   Alack, thou knowest not
How little worthy of any love thou art!
Whom wilt thou find to love ignoble thee,

Save Me, save only Me?
All which I took from thee I did but take,
   Not for thy harms,
But just that thou might'st seek it in My arms.
   All which thy child's mistake
Fancies as lost, I have stored for thee at home:
   Rise, clasp My hand, and come!"

   Halts by me that footfall:
   Is my gloom, after all,
Shade of His hand, outstretched caressingly?
   "Ah, fondest, blindest, weakest,
   I am He Whom thou seekest!
Thou dravest love from thee, who dravest Me."

From the Essay 'Wisdom and the Weather'
(G.K. Chesterton)

   It is admitted, one may hope, that common
things are never commonplace. Birth is covered with
curtains precisely because it is a staggering and
monstrous prodigy. Death and first love, though
they happen to everybody, can stop one's heart with
the very thought of them.

   But while this is granted, something further may
be claimed. It is not merely true that these universal
things are strange; it is moreover true that they are
subtle. In the last analysis most common things will
be found to be highly complicated. Some men of
science do indeed get over the difficulty by dealing

only with the easy part of it; thus they will call first love the instinct of sex, and the awe of death the instinct of self-preservation.

But this is only getting over the difficulty of describing peacock green by calling it blue. There is blue in it. That there is a strong physical element in both romance and the *Memento Mori* makes them if possible more baffling than if they had been wholly intellectual. No man can say exactly how much his sexuality was colored by a clean love of beauty, or by the mere boyish itch for irrevocable adventurism like running away to sea.

No man can say how far his animal dread of the end was mixed up with mystical traditions touching morals and religion. It is exactly because these things are animal, but not quite animal, that the dance of all the difficulties begins. The materialists analyze the easy part, deny the hard part, and go home to their tea.

It is complete error to suppose that because a thing is vulgar, therefore it is not refined; that is, subtle and hard to define. A drawing-room song of my youth which began "In the gloaming, O my darling," was vulgar enough as a song; but the connection between human passion and the twilight is none the less an exquisite and even inscrutable thing.

Or take another obvious instance: the jokes about a mother-in-law are scarcely delicate, but the problem of a mother-in-law is extremely delicate. A mother-in-law is subtle because she is a thing like a twilight. She is a mystical blend of two inconsistent things — law and a mother. The nearest statement of the problem is this: it is not that a mother-in-law must be nasty, but that she must be very nice.

Or to speak of male comradeship. It is obvious that this cool and careless quality which is essential to the collective affection of males involves disadvantages and dangers. It leads to spitting; it leads to coarse speech; it must lead to these things as long as it is honorable; comradeship must be in some degree ugly.

The moment beauty is mentioned in male friendship, the nostrils are stopped with the smell of abominable things. Friendship must be physically dirty if it is to be morally clean. It must be in shirt sleeves. The chaos of habits that always goes with males when left entirely to themselves has only one honorable cure; and that is the strict discipline of a monastery.

Anyone who has seen our unhappy young intellectuals losing their collars in the wash and living on tinned salmon will understand fully why it was decided by the wisdom of St. Bernard and St. Benedict, that if men were to live alone, they must not live without rules.

Something of the same sort of artificial exactitude, of course, is obtained in the army; and an army has to be in many ways monastic; only that it has celibacy without chastity. But these things do not apply to normal married men. These have a quite sufficient restraint on their instinctive anarchy in the savage common-sense of the other sex. There is only one very timid sort of man that is not afraid of women.

From the 1931 Radio Broadcast 'By the Sweat of Thy Brow'
(Father Charles E. Coughlin)

In itself, the law which is expressed in the ancient [adage] "By the sweat of your brow you shall earn your bread" is not sufficient. Nature must be supplemented by supernature, otherwise the handicap under which the weaker live would be too great. "The survival of the fittest," the doctrine that "Might is right" — these would still obtain unless the charity of Jesus Christ had come to our rescue.

Supposing that the governments of modern nations have been anxious to sustain the preliminary law of life as suggested above, what argument could they offer to explain away the catastrophe of the universal breakdown [the Great Depression, 1931] which now confronts us?

Either they have been false to this first principle of all political economy, namely, that bread comes through labor and labor only, or else having practiced and accepted it they are forced to admit that in itself it has not been sufficient.

If the latter is so, then some explanation must be offered both for the causes and the effects which have conspired to make a world grow weary, and so many millions of its people groan in forced idleness.

About sixteen years ago [1914], the first shock of disappointment came thundering upon those of us who believed in the efficacy of our modern, Christless reign of nature. We lived through a war more savage and destructive than ever befell the nations of medieval or barbaric times. We survived through days and years when international law was thrown into the scrap heap. We began to catch a glimpse of our new god of political economy with his feet of clay and his heart of steel.

It was a war to end all wars. But instead of having made the world safe for democracy through the instrumentality of that figment known as the League of Nations, we encounter the results of our mad materialism as they appear today.

Man's noble experiment to make worthwhile progress without Jesus Christ and his principle of charity [has failed completely].

If I were asked to translate this word charity into a simpler word I would use the one single term of "love" — charity is love. First of all it is loving our God with our whole heart, with our whole mind, with our whole strength. It dares not compromise his principles. It is loving our neighbor as ourselves. Not less than ourselves.

The man who would possess real Christian charity must acquire a new concept of his fellow man. He must regard him not merely as a piece of flesh and blood born either to be a slave or a master, a competitor or a protector. He looks beneath the accidental conditions of wealth, of social prestige, of nationality, and catches a glimpse of a real brother.

He is closer in a sense to his fellow man than he is to a brother of his flesh for the simple reason that Jesus Christ, the eldest member of our family, died for all of us without exception and introduced all of us into his common brotherhood by which we can cry out "Abba, Father," to him who created us.

From the Sermon 'Torchbearer of Truth,' in 'The Thoughts of His Heart'
(Bishop Charles Francis Buddy)

You know that zeal for souls is love in action. The poor people, confused and starving for the milk of human kindness, cannot flee from themselves. Only in the truths of Jesus Christ, patiently taught them, will they find peace or hope or stability of heart.

Under the law of Moses, the people gathered to honor and thank almighty God by offering whole burnt offerings. These foreshadowed the adorable

Sacrifice of the Mass which is offered each morning.
In each Holy Mass the celebrant pays highest
worship and the same tribute of thanksgiving to God
as did Jesus Christ when he sacrificed himself upon
the cross of Calvary.

In the Preface for the Mass of the Sacred Heart,
a longing for the "eternal weight of glory" (2 Cor.
4:17) stirs our soul to its very depth when we try to
contemplate the Father almighty, eternal God.

We call on him ". . .everlasting God, who willed
that your only-begotten Son hanging on the cross
should be transfixed with a soldier's lance, so that the
opened heart, treasury of divine bounty, might flood
us with the torrents of compassion and grace; and
that which never ceased to burn with love for us
should be repose for the devout, and to the penitent
should open the shelter of salvation."

Behold the unfathomable goodness, the infinite
mercy of God our Savior. Instead of leaving us
helpless and overwhelmed in the midst of such
obligations, he gave us a means whereby the eternal
Father can be thanked. "What shall I render to the
Lord for all the good things he has given to me? I will
take up the chalice of salvation and I will call upon
the name of the Lord." (Ps. 115:13)

The victim offered to God is his own divine Son
who, in the consecration and communion of the
Mass, is sacrificed in a mystical way. How wonderful
are the gifts of God!

From 'Gaudium et Spes,' No. 39
(Vatican II Documents)

We know neither the moment of the consummation of the earth and of man nor the way the universe will be transformed. The form of this world, distorted by sin, is passing away and we are taught that God is preparing a new dwelling and a new earth in which righteousness dwells, whose happiness will fill and surpass all the desires of peace arising in the hearts of men. Then, with death conquered, the sons of God will be raised in Christ and what was sown in weakness and dishonor will put on the imperishable: charity and its works will remain and all of creation, which God made for man, will be set free from its bondage to decay.

We have been warned, of course, that it profits man nothing if he gains the whole world and loses or forfeits himself. Far from diminishing our concern to develop this earth, the expectancy of a new earth should spur us on, for it is here that the body of a new human family grows, foreshadowing in some way the age which is to come. That is why, although we must be careful to distinguish earthly progress clearly from the increase of the kingdom of Christ, such progress is of vital concern to the kingdom of God, insofar as it can contribute to the better ordering of human society.

When we have spread on earth the fruits of our nature and our enterprise — human dignity, brotherly communion, and freedom — according to the command of the Lord and in his Spirit, we will find them once again, cleansed this time from the stain of sin, illuminated and transfigured, when Christ presents to his Father an eternal and universal kingdom "of truth and life, a kingdom of holiness and grace, a kingdom of justice, love and peace." Here on earth the kingdom is mysteriously present; when the Lord comes it will enter into its perfection.

'Why Do the Innocent Suffer?'
(Joseph Benedict)

Philosophers have pondered this question since they first started to ponder. Why do the innocent suffer?

In general, it is the mystery of free will which makes this all possible. Both love and sin spring from this gift. If we are free to love, we are free to sin, or we are not free at all.

This, then, brings philosophy to the limits of reason and the theologian must take over. Only God could conceive of, and give, such a gift as free will. He respects his gift, and the freedom that helps us reach the heights of ecstasy also lets pride take us down to the depths of hell, to become creatures who can hate, torture, and terrorize.

It is a fact. The innocent frequently suffer, but it can only be explained by the fact of sin, original and actual. Starving children in India and capitalists who corner the grain market are linked by this common humanity.

What, then, when a truly good person suffers a lingering, painful death? If the person were a sinner, then he deserves to suffer. He may well be starting his purgatory here on earth.

But Christ added a whole new meaning to suffering. He, *the* innocent one, suffered to prove his love, to liberate and save sinners. By his suffering, death, and resurrection he freed us from sin and merited — purchased — salvation for all mankind.

Innocent though he was, he became, for us, the Man of Sorrows. His mother, the Immaculata, became the Mother of Sorrows.

Now, we get a glimmer of the value of human suffering. United with Christ's, it has a saving value. The Passion of Christ continues on in the world, calling sinners to repentance.

For some very chosen souls, suffering can be a purifying process, winnowing away the chaff of sin and glorifying the soul. This may be the way for the truly good person to become a great saint.

It is probably not as rare a vocation as some would have us believe. The Passion of Christ continues to save and sanctify the world.

'Pied Beauty'
(Gerard Manley Hopkins)

Glory be to God for dappled things —
    For skies of couple-colour as a brindled cow;
        For rose-moles all in stipple upon trout that
        swim.

Fresh-firecoal chestnut-falls, finches' wings;
    Landscape plotted and pieced — fold, fallow and
        plough;
        And all trades, their gear and tackle trim.

All things counter, original, spare, strange;
    Whatever is fickle, freckled (who knows how?)
        With swift, slow; sweet, sour; a dazzle, dim;

He fathers-forth whose beauty is past change:
    Praise him.

Index